SENESCENCE

SENESCENCE

A YEAR IN THE CANADIAN ROCKIES

AMAL ALHOMSI

RMB

For information on purchasing bulk quantities of this book,
or to obtain media excerpts or invite the author to speak at an
event, please visit rmbooks.com and select the "Contact" tab.

RMB | Rocky Mountain Books Ltd.
rmbooks.com
@rmbooks
facebook.com/rmbooks

Cataloguing data available from Library and Archives Canada
ISBN 9781771607117 (softcover)
ISBN 9781771607124 (electronic)

Copy editor: Kelly Laycock
Cover photo: istockphoto.com/MattGrove

Printed and bound in Canada

We acknowledge the financial support of the Government of Canada
through the Canada Book Fund and the Canada Council for the
Arts, and of the province of British Columbia through the British
Columbia Arts Council and the Book Publishing Tax Credit.

Disclaimer

The views expressed in this book are those of the
author and do not necessarily reflect those of the
publishing company, its staff, or its affiliates.

To my parents, Duaa & Hayyan

To my parents, Dan & Hazel

To try to express oneself and
to want to express the whole of
life are one and the same thing.

—JORGE LUIS BORGES

CONTENTS

CONTENTS

ACKNOWLEDGEMENTS

It is perhaps a blessing that no one bothers with reading acknowledgements, as I am writing it only for you to read. I am so tremendously grateful to every one of you. To Amjad Alhomsi, Bese Birawi, Lucas Prichard, Shoma Mowa, Nico Achondo, and Ji Won Baxter; each of you deserves a novel. Thank you for shaping me and reshaping me throughout the years.

I am also grateful to my teacher German Campus for showing me how to fall in love with literature, and to Natalie Rice and Zach Dewitt for rekindling that love. Most importantly, I am beyond grateful to Annie Dillard for showing me the world.

CHAPTER I

SUMMER

Be friends with your burning.

—RUMI

SENESCENCE

I

I have been waking up like a seashell, hollowed by a departure, tossing between a lapping dream and rumours of morning. I wake up waiting to be turned. My startled neurons scurry like krill to gather whatever self is on the surface. They tuck it under my eyes, knead it behind my ribs. I wake up heaped into desultory memories. I wake up remembering why this bed is my bed, why these walls are my walls, why these hands and this head, then I spend my day trying to forget. I used to fall asleep quicker. I would lie in bed, or on the occasional sofa, and ossify like cheap gum. But things have been different. The body here is at rest, so the mind shakes until it is out of breath.

I live in the Bow Valley, by the Bow River, over the Bow Falls. It is said that it was named so because the people who lived here used to make bows from the reeds that grew on the river's edges, but the river, the trees, the ridges, and the people know that to live in this valley is to be bent like a bow. To sit under these peaks you'll find, slowly in time, your back curving,

your shoulders sinking, as if you've been eroding
against a chinook, as if you've been walking the mountains with the dogs, as if you've been plucked and
twisted with the reeds.

There are two types of people who live here: people
who spend their time in the mountains and people
who are the mountains. The rest are only passing
through. They come to point at the peaks and say,
Look, giant rocks, and then they leave. The river hur-
ries its way out, too, bouncing off shale and limestone,
eating the land like a leaf miner, and leaving a sinuous
trail of trellis drainage. Five mountains surround the
town: Cascade from the north, Sulphur from the south,
Tatanga[1] from the east, Norquay from the northwest,
and Rundle from the southeast. Behind these mountains are more mountains, and behind those mountains, I am told, is the world. If you fly over Calgary
and look west, you will see the peaks hunched like a
herd of sleeping bison – shoulder to shoulder all the
way to Vancouver. They have trampled the continent
into prairies and stopped to rest at its corner, but the
blankets of snow have been receding year after year,
and their torpor might soon be over. In the Book of
Micah, the prophet promises that one day the mountains will melt "like wax before the fire, like water
rushing down a slope."[2] This summer we had the hot-
test June on record. It was so hot I could feel the air
around my neck like a kaffiyeh. Nearly 40°C. Nearly

Riyadh's weather. I would look at a tree and wonder:
How is it not on fire? Is it not just dry sap and timber?
I have never seen things rattle without being touched
by wind. Natalie Rice writes, "Grass is a fire / before it
knows it is a fire."[3] So are the mayflies, so is this body;
lumps of damp mud left until they turn into tar, until
they're burnt out of their clinging. We're not the stuff
of stars. We are, like so much plankton, tarrying in the
crust of Earth until we burst. I dip my feet in glacier
water and sing Tatanga a lullaby.

They

Somewhere in Georgia, a small town is building the
largest topiary statue: a steel chicken that is 62 feet
high with motel rooms in its belly. The project aims
to attract tourism to the quiet town with a slogan that
reads: "If you build it, they will cluck." The construc-
tion cost the town nearly US$300,000. Jim Puckett,
the mayor of the town, was thrown out of office before the chicken was given its verdant feathers.[4] Now
its skeleton haunts the side of the road like a totem. It
is not clear why Puckett built a chicken rather than,
say, a cow or a hedgehog. It is not clear why Puckett
built the chicken at all. Perhaps, like Noah, he was told
something we weren't. Regardless, the chicken is there,
and it is there so people who pass by might point at it
and say, *Look! A giant chicken!*

Then

Since the beginning, people have been anticipating an end. Narratives of apocalypse are older than stories of genesis. In *The Epic of Gilgamesh*, the earliest surviving work of literature, antediluvian memories permeate the epic. The narrator remembers a flood that came and washed mankind into nothing, while the Torah speaks of a day where "not a root or a branch will be left," where everything "will burn like a furnace."[5] Christianity, with its many denominations, foretells the Great Tribulation, the Rapture, Armageddon, and a time when "nation will rise against nation, and kingdom against kingdom, and there will be famines and earthquakes in various places."[6] The Buddhist *Aṅguttara Nikāya* scripture prophesies a season when "all seedlings, all vegetation, all plants, grasses and trees will dry up and cease to be."[7] It is everywhere, and everyone knows it. They have planted the universe too many times and watched it die. It is sprouted like a seed, married into one, and spoken until evinced. Then, the season, the hate, the silence…And from then on, it is all ceasing, withering, dispersing. Death is handed to you with every "*Hello, have you heard about our way of life?*"

Geologist Mike Hulme writes, "The human imagination seems to engage with [the] future in a way that oscillates between deep despair and the hope of salvation."[8] In the Quran, Allah warns in three consecutive verses, "Lo! the punishment of thy Lord is stern. Lo! It is He who originates and repeats. And He is the All-Forgiving, All-Loving."[9] Punishment and love, like death and regeneration, are offered in the same breath. There is death in the promise of salvation, death in the prophecy of a new beginning, and death in the act of mere living. There is also an urgency to it. Whether it is Greek mythology or Zoroastrian eschatology, the Kali Yuga or Al-akhira, tomorrow or a hundred years ago, the end is as near as a vein to the skin. Don't press. Sooner or now, the ebb will come without the flow, and we will be flooded with nothingness and left with nothing to carry us, or so I'm told.

Around 1830, Baptist preacher William Miller intensively studied the visions of Daniel that warned the end of Earth "will take 2,300 evenings and mornings."[10] Miller, with scientific precision, scrutinized the evidence and compared the results. He concluded that 2,300 days are 2,300 years, due to Ezekiel's explanation of "one day for each year." And since God promised that transgression in Jerusalem would end in "seventy sevens,"[11] Miller decided on 457 BCE to be the beginning of the end, as it was the year when the king of Persia empowered the prophet Ezra to ordain order. He then calculated seventy weeks as the first 490 years of the 2,300 years and added to the sum the years that followed, bringing him to the final answer that the cleansing of the world would happen

on October 22, 1844. Millerites sold their houses, re-
signed from their positions, and waited in anticipation for the world to be washed, to be turned. Miller
stayed in his house, holding his hands together, praying for the hands of the clock to part quicker. Did he
wait with doubt and fear? Did his mind go in circles,
or did he drink tea? There is nothing I want to know
more. What does one do while waiting for the beast to
rise from the sea "with ten horns and seven heads,"[12]
for the dragon to split the earth back open, for the sun
to turn as "black as sackcloth" and the full moon to
be soaked with blood,[13] for the flood to swallow us
all? But the waiting needed more waiting. Who knows
what God thinks? That October day came and went,
and in the morning the birds hovered with life. Miller,
and his people, woke up, if they had slept at all, to a
great disappointment.

In his 1968 book, *The Population Bomb*, biologist
Paul R. Ehrlich predicted for hundreds of millions
of people to starve to death in the '70s and a nuclear war to occur in the '80s. We were warned by scientists that between 1983 and 1993, we would run out
of gold, copper, petroleum, zinc, and natural gas. We
were timed, like a crème brûlée, to burn out after a
time. Yet, somehow, we are still here, cracking the
oven door open every once in a while to reset the
clock. Ten more minutes before we're done, or maybe
twenty, or maybe someone misread the recipe. No god

has tried his people more than time, and no prophet has disappointed his people more than science.
Roy Scranton, in *Learning to Die in the Anthropocene*,
writes of "rising seas, spiking temperatures, and extreme weather...Conflict, famine, plagues, and
riots,"[14] which sounds like a prophecy from the Book
of Matthew. There seems to be no ingenuity in death.
"Dying" as Sylvia Plath knew, "is an art."[15] But if we
compare eschatologies, even the most innovative are
reiterative. Suns swallowed by wolves and Magog eating Earth, a few years of plagues and a monsoon. Then
what? There is always, no matter how drastic the dis-
aster, a messiah, an ark, a second sun, a new planet,
or a sapling that survived the trampling. The end is
only about a beginning, a sort of resetting, a return
to zero, a reversing of entropy. Even in our wildest
dreams we are still cowards. There is no end to our
end. Seneca blames the stars: "All that the earth inher-
its will be consigned to flame when the planets, which
now move in different orbits, all assemble in Cancer...
When the same gathering takes place in Capricorn,
then we are in danger of the deluge."[16]

We have always been turning between a burning and
a deep drowning, as if death knows no other way to
get rid of us. Fate carries our feet, and all we can do is
walk and weep, but how can one choose how to live if
he can't choose how to die? What am I to do with what
I was given if taking it or leaving it is not an option?

Even Plato believed that one day the planets would return to their original places only to repeat their cycle
again, and since the Greeks tied the unfolding of their
days to the positions of the stars, a cyclical astral sys-
tem meant a cyclical human history. Soon, Odysseus
will set sail on his galley to Ithaca, Caesar will touch
Cleopatra's nose, and the Serengeti will grow back
again, and I will lose a molar to a hill, a hat to the wind.
Tomorrow, I will count to ten and join a circus. I might
pretend to be a man with dark hair and then show the
constellations my balding head. I might trick my star
out of its orbit. Because I am desperate to know that
what I live has never been lived before, and I am willing to risk some hair for it. Maybe then I might escape
this entanglement. Francis Bacon tells us "all knowledge was but remembrance" and "all novelty is but
oblivion."[17] Tomorrow and yesterday are hidden in
one another. Five mass extinctions already occurred
in the history of Earth, three of which were caused by
giant floods, but one was the result of photosynthe-
sis that suffocated the planet. Our precious oxygen,
Frederick W. Turner observes, "is the toxic waste of
the first polluters."[18] Even the Cambrian explosion, an
event celebrated as the beginning of life, paradoxically marked the first "mass death in the history of complex life."[19] Like the Ouroboros serpent eating its tail,
nature renews itself by destroying itself. Behold, "old
things are passed away; behold, all things are become

new."[20] Was there ever a prophet who, after shivering
from some afflatus, dragged his ripped rags up a hill
and preached that in the beginning was the word, and
the word was the world, and the word is final? What
would we, after crucifying him, have done?

Them

There is more information on how to kill a leaf miner than on how to understand one. How do they get
into the leaves? *Install fine mesh-netting covers to protect the plants.* How long do they live inside a leaf?
Introduce parasitic wasps to eat the eggs. What's their
eye colour? *Make a DIY white oil using vinegar and
dish soap to spray the infected spots.* Why is it difficult
to know something without having to kill it first?

On the sides of the Bow River, if you look closely,
you'll find various berry shrubs with leaves that look
like a ball-in-a-maze puzzle, eaten, or mined, by larvae
known as leaf miners. The miners belong to numerous
species of insects that lay their eggs in leaves so that
the newly hatched larvae will wake up to a guaranteed
meal. They open their colourless eyes to a life promised only through death, so they chew their birthplace,
leaving its outer layers and its pillars intact, until the
leaf dies. The miners hurry their way out, bouncing
off tissue and mesophyll, and then fall like a river into
an infinite green ocean, an ocean that awaits their devouring. The meandering tunnels left behind seem

almost familiar, like ancient cuneiform, or prehistoric petroglyphs on the ceiling of some cave. I can look at them. I can trace their decay with my fingers. I can even give them names, but I can never know what they mean. I often collect the leaves to see if any two have a similar pattern to them. I want to find my Rosetta leaf. I want to crack the code. I want to catch God idling, to point at the chiselling hand and say, "Aha!" But the patterns are always new, always beautiful.

You

In the beginning, I dreamt you and you appeared, and we saw that it was good, so you took 25 years of your life and anchored them with a toothbrush in my bathroom. You were never really there, and I never really saw you. Our bed, with its marigold floral sheet, wasn't there, nor your lipsticks by the sink, nor your hair in the folds of my shirt. I knew you only with my fingers, as crevices and lumps and wrinkles. The height of your nape. The shape of your shoulders. But then the season, the hate, the lapping. It should've been bearable, but our oscillation had no Holocene. I think I might have promised you the punishment and forgot the love, and I think you might have loved me wrong and hated me right, but that's all right, because we were never really there. Take a handful of sand and swallow it. It'll taste only like sand.

I

David Foster Wallace said once that an artist must be willing to risk the yawn. And here it is risked on every turn of the head. The repeated lines of spruces, the implausible clouds, the reiterated detail of every prickly bead of grass. Wallace also dreamt of a world that happens, as opposed to a world that happens to us. But alas, you can't have everything that you wish for. I walk around town to see who the streets are happening to. Summer spills here like a blob of honey, and sudden armies of crawling creatures swarm the small sweetness. Dippers and jays fly from above, groundhogs from underneath, and people over the surface of Earth. "The number of them," true to Revelation's prediction, "is like the sand of the seashore."[21] When the sun is up, they come out from the corners of the earth. They fall down the avenue like an avalanche to eat the land with their feet, the sky with their teeth, and the lakes with their bare shoulders. "Behold, I am against you."[22] Behold, I am you. Who knew? Life and death are not wings to the same bird. They are the bird itself – not carried but carrying. Of course, it wasn't always like this. There used to be two worlds, one made of fingers and walls, and another made of nothing at all. When the latter would be confronted with the loss of something, it would shatter into itself like a star, and we would become frozen in time, and the moment would become all moments, and the place all places, but that was the other world's beauty, its seasons, migrations, and rotation were reasons enough to remind us that – by virtue of all things that crawl and breathe and bounce – we, too, can move on. It was our greatest healing that the worm came out of the earth in the summer, and the snow buried our windows in the winter. What do we do now when our loss is the loss of that healing? Next summer, how do we recover, if both love and the worms leave us?

They

There are five reasons why owning a yacht can benefit the environment, or so claims the article, "Why Yachting Families Make Great Climate Caretakers."[23] First, a yachting family is able to "bear witness" to the dying ocean. Watching marine life choke on plastic straws "is not just something adults can do onboard, but is an activity that children can join in with too." Unlike other families, yachting families can point at a decaying coral reef and say, *Look, it's decaying!* Second, when environmentalists need a ride to "hard-to-reach areas," they can hitch a ride on a yacht, and the children can meet them and "develop a love of science and climate protection." Third, yachting families can tag, track, and adopt marine animals to help with documentation. Fourth, when climate disasters occur, yachting families can offer their yachts to help transfer those in need. Afterall, "weather-related disasters are only set to increase as the planet warms, and we will need all of those who have the resources to offer their support." Finally, when a yacht is no longer need-ed, it can be recycled into other maritime industries. Superyacht owners are not only "investing in their fu-tures, but in the future of the planet too."

Then

In the early 1800s, an Italian astronomer predicted that the sun would go out and that Earth would freeze in eternal darkness. Like all prophets, he was ridiculed, and like all prophets, he was half right. In 1815, the sun did disappear, and a wave of mysterious weather swept Earth, causing droughts and famines in China, abnormal warmth in Japan, and cold and wet sum-mers in Europe. Some parts of the world were com-pletely in the dark for a few months. It took people 150 years to understand that the global climatic disrup-tion was caused by the eruption of Mount Tambora in Indonesia. The mountain emitted an ash cloud large enough to veil the sun and lower the global temper-ature, resulting in the year known as the Year with-out Summer. The tephra in the air obscured the world, inspiring an art movement that would not have hap-pened otherwise. Artists began to write and paint a world that they believed was reaching its end, giving us a glimpse of Miller's mind. Caspar David Friedrich painted sepia skies and dreary sunsets, Mary Shelley

wrote *Frankenstein*, and Byron dreamt in his famous
poem "Darkness":

> The bright sun was extinguish'd, and the stars
> Did wander darkling in the eternal space,
> Rayless, and pathless, and the icy earth
> Swung blind and blackening in the moonless air...

The darkness made people search for something to
believe in, and Prometheus, bringer of light, was the
needed prophet of many a generation. Works of art
over the centuries have paid tribute to his name in their
titles: Beethoven's ballet *The Creatures of Prometheus*,
Aeschylus's drama *Prometheus Bound*, Goethe's poem
"Prometheus," and Shelly's alternative title to her novel
Frankenstein, The Modern Prometheus.[24] But the
world, as the beating of your heart will insist, did not
end. More years came, and more predictions came
with them, and more mythologies followed to justify it
all. It is our favourite game to play; to try and explain
non-human events with human terms. An eclipse
used to appear as a goddess, then as a muse, and now
it happens as a fact. Modernity's mythology is its science. When the flood seeped from cracks in the sky,
preachers blamed it all on our sins; when the sun lost
its orbit, the poets assured us that it was due to our
lack of humanity; and when the world began to melt
like wax before the fire, scientists showed us how the
problem is our greed and gluttony. We're all walking

around with our heads looking up and our eyes diz-
zied by the same clouds, some auguring a future while
others exorcizing ghosts of the past. The conclusion
remains unanimous: the fault, like a bone, is within
us. But if so, where would the solution be? Do we, like
the bird, carry both on each side? Or are we forced
by some astral alignment to never look behind? Yukio
Mishima thought that humans are stranger than any
other animal because they have the ability to de-
file with one hand and make miracles with the other.
Perhaps it's time for us to choose a hand, to lose a bone.

Them

The birds are here only to prove us wrong. Their small
hearts and gentle halluces make no dents in the sky,
their quiet fluttering and light feathers have no weight
against the clouds. You can hardly tell that they are
there. Long ago, they were all there was – terrible reptiles that pressed the earth into shape – but now we
know them only by bones.

We are told that the largest dinosaurs reached almost
18 metres in height. We are also told that they spent
around 165 million years living – if you want to call
what they did living. That's almost 36,000 times longer than humans have been around. That's 165 million
years of chewing and breathing and populating only
for them to end up at a museum where children point
at them and say, *Look, giant bones!* And that's not even

all of them. Some dinosaurs, the ones who lived in the late Jurassic period, which spanned 18 million years, exist, like Santa Claus, only as a necessary story; no trace whatsoever remains of them. As for the pieces of bones that the earth agreed to keep, we look for them on the banks of rivers, we give them names (ankylosaur and ceratopsian and ornithopod), we trace their history (Triassic and Jurassic and Cretaceous), but can we know what they mean? The Chinese thought them to be dragons and cooked them in medicinal soups. The Europeans believed them to be the remains of biblical giants and turned them into a paste for bone ache. And now we are told that they were reptiles wiped out by a giant celestial rock.

Regardless of who you want to believe, consider the sparrow outside your window, barely noticeable, crumbling like a honey cake against every breeze, but when it flies up, it does so despite the chaos of memories, unmoved by the unpredictable vastness. And in the morning, or even at dusk, when the sun, like an asteroid, peels the edges of the sky, you'll hear them chirping. But they're only gloating – I am I am I am more than what you leave.

I

A friend of mine who volunteers as a live model for drawing classes told me why she does it. She said it happens every session, right in the middle, or just at the moment when the artists had limned her outlines and are now faced with her face, the artists, vacantly, will look at the model's eyes and then shudder. They realize, one by one, that what they are looking at is looking back at them.

A vireo swoops by my eye to catch a worm, then disappears somewhere behind a pine. The waterfall with all its busied hands guides the current away from the banks. A magpie watches a squirrel who is testing the faithfulness of a branch. I wait with a book on my lap for the day to come up with something new, but the vireo swoops by to catch a butterfly, the water murmurs something then turns around, and the squirrel is now looking at a magpie who is too tired to sing. The world is waiting to be turned, and none of it remembers me. I look it in the eyes, I push my face against its face, but I don't shudder. When I was 8, my mother, with a knife in her hand and my head on her lap, would feed me sweet strawberries and recite the names of God to me. With every name she uttered, I received a perfectly circular slice of strawberry. Al-rahman, strawberry slice. Al-manan, strawberry slice. Al-salam, and so on. God has 99 names and a strawberry punnet has eight strawberries, yet, somehow, she made it work. After every punnet, to affirm the monotheism she strictly adhered to, she would finish by saying: "God is one, like no one, and greater than everyone." The sweetness was in my mouth. The content was in her heart. All she wanted was to be God-like. What a mission to set yourself on, to want to be someone who is no one.

A few years ago, a company edited the genes of strawberries to make them require less water to grow. Scientists have also genetically modified potatoes by switching off the genes that cause them to brown when exposed to oxygen, successfully cross-bred onions that do not carry tear-jerking chemicals, and grew seedless watermelons by playing cat's cradle with their genes. They, too, were on the same mission. On one of the pages of the book I'm reading, I sketch two stones leaning into one another, the boughs shaking in the air like wet dogs, the sleeping magpie, the riverbank and the leaf miners and the shadows in between. The whole scene holds together, but what am I doing here? Someone should've told us, and my mother should've known, to be like God is to be alone.

They & Them Back Then

At some point in history, nothing at all happened, but we will never know that. Time, like the sky, is unobservable unless there are some constellations to mark it, some dots that we can point at and name. We, regular folks, remember history like a dream. The specialists, however, look at history anatomically. They etherize the past like a toad, cut it open with a scalpel, stick their finger in and feel the lumps. Do you notice the ice age at the tip of the tongue? They do. They

know why the frog leaps, how it sleeps. They even
know how many flies a week it eats – none. The dead
don't eat a thing.

During 1884, before Banff was given its name, geologist George Mercer Dawson was travelling around
Western Canada dissecting and pointing and feeling
the lumps. Wherever he went, his name followed like
a plague: Dawson Creek and Dawson City. Dawson,
however, was not necessarily interested in the usual
espièglerie of European explorers. He was more fo-
cused on charting the vastness, on dotting the empty
map for his fingers to prove to his feet that the earth
he is standing on does exist. He learned the languages
of the people he met and recorded their cultures with
genuine attentiveness. But it happens involuntari-
ly. Adam's hubris is inherited like a surname. When
Dawson saw a few caribou on Haida Gwaii, the species, merely by being gazed at, was immediately named
Dawson's caribou, even though Dawson himself did
not name it. He, however, did misname it – a taxo-
nomical error that proved fatal. In the 291-page report
that Dawson wrote about the islands, the caribou is
mentioned only in a brief sentence: "There is pretty
good evidence to show that the wapiti occurs on the
northern part of Graham Island, but it is very seldom
killed."[25] Wapiti is commonly known as elk. Dawson,
perhaps after learning from the Haida People, later
corrected his report to say caribou instead of wapiti.

By changing the name, Dawson sentenced the species
to the most bizarre extinction, a death by a demand to
provide evidence of life.

Caribou usually inhabit dry lands, whereas Dawson's
caribou dwelt in unsuitably humid areas, and the scientific community wanted proof of the existence of
such caribou. They wanted something to feel with
their fingers. The demand for evidence incentivized
a reward, the rewards encouraged a market, and the
market, in the name of science, resulted in wiping out
the already rare species. A few skeletons made their
way to universities across the nation. Scientists poked
the bones, measured them against their arms, and
put them in museums. Some found the evidence con-
vincing, others objected that it was inconclusive, as
the bullets had destroyed the skulls, and others even
doubted the story all together, accusing the Haida of
bringing the caribou from Alaska for the sake of the
reward. The debate continued, and more bones were
brought to be stretched on tables. Until, in 1908, a
family of Dawson's caribou were shot and presented
to the scientific community that resolved all doubts
about the existence of this reclusive animal. At the de-
cisive moment that scientists confirmed the existence
of the caribou, they declared its extinction. The caribou family proved to be the last surviving herd on the
islands.

Curiosity killed the caribou, but satisfaction brought

us back for more. In 1964, a graduate student named Donald R. Currey found Prometheus, a bristlecone pine tree that was possibly more than 5,000 years old. Currey, oblivious to the age of the tree, wanted to find out how long a non-clonal organism can live for. He also wanted to see what the insides of the tree would tell him about the little ice age. Currey cut Prometheus open with a chainsaw, stuck his fingers in, and counted the rings. To his shock, Prometheus had been standing there 4,000 years before the little ice age had started. What Currey discovered was something we already knew, an oblivion he remembered; the mind waits in circles, in rings that grow until they are turned. Parts of the tree now can be found displayed in national parks and museums, next to dinosaur bones and stuffed dodos, where visitors point at them and say, *Look, 4,900 years!*

You

I knew it would be easy to find you, to point at some pebbles and say that we existed there for a few hours, to trace the banks of the Bow and hear you echoing. I knew, too well, that if I came back here, if I ripped the memories open with a cup of tea and looked for you, that I would find you everywhere. I know all your favourite birds, how long it takes before I tire you, and how many dreams you have a week. I'm not sure why I came back. Perhaps, like the zealous, I was looking for a new sapling, or for someone to drive an axe through this circling. How strange it is that Hiroshima never happened, nor did the Armenian genocide. Trauma, according to Cathy Caruth, is known belatedly and occurs only after our departure from it.[26] Trauma can only be lived through remembrance, through traces and dots that point to fictions of the original event. The moment itself is inaccessible, beyond reach, yet all that I've been doing, all that we've been doing, is reaching. Few strands of your hair are in the folds of my blanket, a picture of you in a red swimming suit on my bedroom wall, and a small cut on my thigh from when you were drunk; this is your museum that I imagined if I built you would cluck, but I have too many walls and too much skin. What would happen if I spent a day in the kitchen? I think I've been stuck between the arrival and the departure. I think I've been waiting for you like a Millerite in October. George Bernard Shaw remarked once that learning something always feels at first like losing something. I have nothing left to lose after these years of learning how to lose you. But in the morning when I wake up, a siskin bird, barely noticeable, is here, and so are my hands, so is my head.

All of Us, Here & Now

Geologically speaking, we have never existed. Our history, scaled in deep time, is not long enough to leave a dent, to mark a dot. The earliest readings in the earth were composed 4.55 billion years ago, readings that can come with 50,000-year error bars. That's all our poetry, mountains, nuclear bombs, plastic straws, cave paintings, and gods outlived by an error bar. What will a few centuries of us chewing the surface do? Yahweh, after weeks of listening to Job's frustrations, responded simply by asking, "Where wast thou when I laid the foundations of the earth?"[27] It's a good question, but a rude thing to say. If my grief, in the grand scheme of things, doesn't matter, then why should my sins? Can I drink my coffee without thinking about Peru? We're only a season, a thin ring in that tree that no one has yet to cut down. It's not Earth, it's us who are dying, or so I am told. But back then, the world was old, and it moved slowly. What took years to do can now be done in a day. We were born yesterday, but we're moving as fast as a meteorite. If our life and loud breathing was the child of the waste left from a death before us, then what beauty will come out of this burning? In this raging heat, over our hungry shoulders, the surface and the crust are vanishing, but the pillars are still intact, the foundations are visible, and as I feel the fall coming, I close my eyes and open my mouth, because maybe, I might swear by a leaf miner, there is freedom in gluttony. And maybe, while falling, while fleeing, our hands will grow wings, and our feet will learn to walk without noise. Or maybe we, like the shilly-shallying shimmer of a lapsed sun, have died long ago and are now only rushing blindly, palpitating desperately out of an end that preceded us, hoping to fall under fingers that could name us into some meaning. But who knows what a star thinks?

On this June night, I point at the tarrying glow of atoms freed from crushing bodies into a nothingness that is forever and for good, and I whisper, *Look, a passing light!* We've cut down Prometheus, and we've been burning for some time now, and all that our prophets can do is point and weep, and all that we are will be nothing more than strands lost in the folds of the earth, a voice barely whispering in the memory of the oceans. I have learnt, while losing my mind, that there is freedom in departure. I have been waiting, while bending my edges, for my senescence like an ocean, between a circle of fire and flooding sand. But now I might go east, where fruit is cheaper, and buy myself some strawberries. I might seep, little by little, out of this heavy shell into infinite blue waters.

GHOSTS

Sometimes in space, and out of nowhere, two galaxies become entangled in one another. Stars and moons and emptiness begin to "dance around each other in circles that become smaller and smaller."[28] For millions of years, this galactic entanglement pirouettes and crashes into itself until it becomes nothing, and for millions of years, the collision produces the loudest noise the universe is capable of making, yet has anyone ever heard it? It passes like a ghost. Behind the spruce, the magpie's shrill is louder than the sun, and all I see here is light. All I see is light. The world believes in ghosts, in black holes and big bangs and boson particles. If I turn my eyes upwards, I can calmly be possessed. July is when Earth forgets its age. Senile skies and tattered trees are masqueraded with youthfulness. Everything seems as old as today, and every day is as nascent as now. There is not a single leaf that is other than a gorgeous green, and the heaving lungs of the forest inhale the sun whole. It's a brashness we're too familiar with: for a birch to rise every dawn and hold on with its being to something it knows will eventually go. "The flowers growing in the

desolation of Mount St. Helens," historian Frederick
W. Turner observes, "testify to what in human beings
we would call a lunatic hopefulness, the optimism of
the amateur."[29] Lately, I have been feeling young, and
my dark hair against the sun's flare grows like lichen.
Summer is a fable which all the living believe, so why
should I, no wiser than a larch, doubt. I wear my hair
like a mountain heather.

On the Spray River, a muskrat waddles with a twig
between its teeth. Water striders wear the air like bowl-
ing shoes and glide until they knock some mosquito
larvae. A coween on its way to the Arctic dives for a
dragonfly, its sharp, palmated feet a *hara-kiri* against
the soft surface. Everything is on the move. I only sit
on the bank and watch. There is barely anything in
me that wants to stay in me. Ibn Rushd once asked
that if we were made of water, would we have known
things differently. The name Adam is derived from the
Hebrew *adamah*, meaning "from the earth." And the
Hebrew for soul is *nafs*, which can translate to "wind."
Of the four elements, only earth is capable of confin-
ing, and only wind flows without restriction. We are
a contradiction; a *nafs* that is consistently at work to
erode its *adamah*. If I were made of water, every mol-
ecule of me sprawling, I would go with the muskrat, I
would know the river, but if I wish like a tree to hold,
would I want then what I want now? My fingers are
too thin, anyways.

On the bank of the Bow I was duped. The world seemed still until it wasn't. What use is a root if the earth it's embedded in keeps spinning. This motion without consent is dizzying. You open a book and blink a few times, and, before you know it, you are now where Mongolia was. A sea sponge, after nestling in a good spot, will move two millimetres an hour simply by breathing. In the morning I inhaled, and there was a terrible noise; currents and killdeer and cudweed against the wind. Now there's a fire near, and ash is riding the air like snow. I have done nothing but breathe, and the noise is now numb. Smog has a silence like ice, like blood. I have done it again; I came here to test the waters, then I was knee-deep in time, then I was swallowed.

***

Some decades ago, at exactly 4:00 a.m., a miner from the town of Frank looked outside his kitchen window where Turtle Mountain stood centred between his orange mullions. In the time it took him to boil a cup of coffee, 110 million tonnes of limestone rock the size of 30 million cubic metres broke off from the peak of the mountain and fell on the eastern side of the town, killing around 70 people. Geologists still speculate on why the mountain decided to move all of a sudden. The entire plate that makes up much of British Columbia is swimming northward, migrating away from the continent it had called home for millions of years. The peaks of the Rockies, which were once the bottom of an ocean, will become prairies one day. Things don't move all of a sudden; things never cease to move at all. To be steady as a rock is to be forever agitated. There is coral in the clouds, stardust in the ocean, and cats in airplane engines.[30]

Sometimes on the west coast of North America, and out of nowhere, a mysterious phenomenon called sea star wasting syndrome begins to occur. It starts with the sea star refusing food. Then, with time, the star loses colour and disintegrates until its edges turn into a circle, and the circle into nothingness. Sea stars don't move much. They reside on the same earth for years and make a home out of it, until, for reasons unknown to us, the star collapses into itself – without making a sound – and disappears. What do they get entangled with? There are ghosts that gnaw, churning and withering and wave-lapping. There are glaciations and exfoliations and avalanches. I am here, still, by the river, sitting on a crooked branch, and in the thick smog I glimpse a monarch butterfly. I chase it until I lose it somewhere, until I find it nowhere. When I told Lucas about it, he laughed at me. "Monarchs have no business being here," he said. "The smoke probably got to your head." When I arrived at the park three summers ago, there was a fire then, too, and I, far from the home I lost, found myself in the middle of nowhere. I miss it there, but it's taking me all my life to wait for my life to begin. How many cups of coffee must I make for a home to fall by my window? Or will I sit here until this stillness turns me inside out?

In the '80s, a small Syrian town called Hama woke up to smoke. Hafez al-Assad, the Syrian president at the time, had received rumours of a coup d'état and didn't want to gamble his odds. He summoned a cartographer and asked him to redraw the map of Syria. The new map was to be an exact replica barring a single alteration; the town of Hama was to be erased from the map, omitted from the world. Reports vary, but it is estimated that somewhere between 20,000 and 40,000 Hama residents perished that day. The events were one of the deadliest acts by any Arab government against its own people. The army was told to go shoot all that moves. But soldiers follow orders, not metaphors. Carcasses of cats and pigeons and rats were heaped on sidewalks. When reading the names of the deceased from the archives, one will notice that most are grouped according to their family names. This is not due to a methodical recording. The massacre happened in the morning, and the dead happened to be grouped around the breakfast table; daughter by her father, and brother by his brother. A week after, a third of the population was either dead, missing, or had fled the town. Some women were spared due to an odd sense of chivalry, one of whom managed to hide her son under her orange dress. When her husband was shot in front of her, she stayed still for the sake of the life clinging to her damp thighs. From the seams of the dress, the child watched his father's blood running down the floor. It was orange.

Every fall, millions of North American monarch butterflies migrate to seek refuge in the warmer southern parts of the continent. The location of their overwintering grounds remained unknown until 1975 when Kenneth Brugger and his wife Catalina stumbled upon it in the mountains of central Mexico. Fred Urquhart, a Canadian zoologist who led the Bruggers' search party, was looking for the overwintering spots for more than 38 years. He announced the discovery of the site in the 1976 issue of *National Geographic*, a site the local Mexicans had known about for generations. Sometimes every November, tens of thousands of monarchs arrive to cover the trees at Michoacán. Their orange tint replaces the green of the leaves. They huddle in clusters to keep warm as they fall and return to the same branch like an eternal autumn. These overwintering butterflies are called super monarchs. Their bodies weigh less than a piece of gum and their wingspan is smaller than a thumb, yet they travel an average distance of 4500 kilometres from north to south. When March approaches, their wings soak in the heat and begin to uncurl like tulips, then they cascade out of trees flooding the forest. But butterflies do not have the lifespans of birds. The super monarch that crossed seas and cities must die before it returns home, so it lays its eggs on milkweed and flutters softly to its death. A lifeless blanket of orange covers the grounds of Michoacán's forest. The newly hatched larvae feed on the milkweed, pupate, and emerge to become the second generation of monarchs. They open their eyes to flee from the dawning of winter.

In the winter of 1944, after remaining neutral throughout the war, the Netherlands decided, suddenly, to move. Dutch railway workers refused to transport Nazi troops through the Netherlands in the hope of aiding the Allied Forces. But the Allied Forces failed, and Germany planned to punish the Dutch with a blockade of food and fuel. The year became known as the Hongerwinter. People burnt furniture to keep warm and ate tulip bulbs to stay alive, but they ran out of tulips quicker than chairs. Twenty-two thousand people died from starvation. During the famine, exactly 2,414 babies were born, all of whom were small and slender. They were called the Dutch Famine Birth Cohort. It was a shock to no one that children born after a famine would be born malnourished, but when those children grew up and had children of their own, their babies were also born smaller than the average baby size. Geneticists speculate: How did the newborns carry their grandparents' hunger after all these years?

After all these years, we are still, like windowsills, unable to hold the light, to stop the turning, to believe the noise. In Zeno's paradox, the arrow only exists when it's moving, but its moving is not possible without infinite thresholds that haunt its stillness. Ghosts do not exist, they resist. Neither here nor there, neither willing to leave nor accepting to stay, neither moving nor moved, they hold our world while we pass them like an arrow.

After the massacre of Hama, the other Syrian towns went quiet. al-Assad's scare tactic worked impeccably. No one wanted to be erased from a map, and Hama became neither here nor there. In time, grass grew over the mass graves, jasmine filled the bullet holes in the hammams and ottoman houses, some walls were painted red to mask the tinge of blood, and the norias of Hama kept spinning to the tune of a song that played from every radio, "Spin, spin, o noria, and forget about the past." And people did. Children played soccer over their uncles' graves, farmers invented a forest fire that swallowed their farms, and those who remembered the past and told it disappeared into secret prisons. As for my father, he told me neither a truth nor a lie. He only said that he hated the colour orange.

Clouds of orange butterflies leave Mexico and follow their parents' path northward. It remains a mystery how the newly hatched generation knows exactly where to return to; do they wear their mother's worry like a compass, or do their wings inherit a heaviness that can only be itched by flying north? The air in Syria seemed always heavy with a silence about to fester, and the generation that was born from the massacre was haunted by a past that shaped their bones. The new generation is weak and small. Their delicate wings cannot handle the weight of their parents' burden. They die along the way after laying another generation of migrants. The ghost of the monarch that was born in Mexico will arrive at its mother's birthplace only after four or five generations. My cousin's son arrived in Syria 40 years after his grandfather died. He set fire to a tire and rolled it at the grandsons of the sentries that burnt his house. His bones were itching until they were shattered by a sniper's bullet. Hafez al-Assad was long dead, but when his son Bashar was born, he was more malignant than the average child. Life, as Jack London claimed, is movement. The circle keeps turning until it turns to nothing. The last monarchs reach home and give birth to yet another generation of super monarchs that wake up haunted by an urge for warmth. It's been ten years since the second Syrian civil war began, and now everyone is closing their eyes. It's time for torpor. Come summer, the bodies will be warm again. If Lucas was right, then I, too, have no business being here, putting roots in desolation, growing with anticipation into a circle. Some nights the ghosts gnaw, and they tangle my blood, and

I feel a pull loud enough to be inaudible, but where
would I, half earth, half frost, go? I'll crumble. I'll be
out without a word. Soon this blur, and the tug and
the jitter, and the spinning of the zephyr will all attest.
I have witnessed a miracle; I took my sandals off, and
I walked on nothing.

TAWAF

He washes under cold water and his sins clog the drain. Blocks of black *bakhoor* burn by the mirror filling the bathroom with the scent of the Kaaba. The faint voice of a Yemeni child reciting the beginning *surahs* plays from the radio of the white taxi parked outside the building; "Aleph Lam Meem. This is the book in which there is no doubt." No one knows what Aleph Lam Meem means. It is the first verse in the Quran. The faith begins with doubt, and the doubt is followed by a reassurance that there is no doubt, so he smiles at the merited arrogance. The water swirls around his feet, the steam around the ventilation fan, and his thoughts around God. Our mother wanted me to be with him. "You've been hiding from God long enough," she said. He turns the tap off and shrouds his nakedness with two cotton cloths without ornaments. His bare feet collect blessings as they walk on the footsteps of Muhammad. Muhammad is the most common name in the world. It is also the name of the taxi driver. "The road to Mecca is not paved," says Muhammad, "so driving feels like riding a camel."

"The road is worse than the streets of Calgary," says

the bus driver as he maneuvers up rugged hills. The passengers stretch their necks searching for the promise of scenery. There are twelve of us riding a green school bus. An American man with yellow binoculars is talking to a lady sitting behind him. I know he is American because he starts each sentence by saying "I." "I am single," he says, "I can tolerate hostels and hitch-hikers." An old man in the back hums a song about sleeping buffalos. The bus stutters around the silence of the mountains, and birds burst out of the earth like boiling water. There is nothing to see on the road but trees standing tall like a million Alephs. Is this the doubt before the belief? We stop at an orange sign reading LAKE O'HARA. Our guide lists the rules of camping and mentions something about the weather. "Make sure to try the carrot cake at the tea house," she says, "it's the world's best." I know she is not Canadian because she only smiles when she means it. The twelve of us circle the campsite searching for an earth to sleep on for the next three days.

He munches on some dates that the taxi driver gave him. The dates of Medina are unparalleled; they taste like caramelized chocolate-honey. The call of prayer travels on the backs of pigeons as big as cats. God is greater. God is greater. Mecca smells like pigeons, like feet and Ethiopian beggars, like Himalayan musk and cheap henna, like faces washed with Zamzam and tiles washed with tears, like Persian carpets, roasted chickpeas, and prophets. He wants to run to the Kaaba and drown in the crowd behind Abraham's stone. He wants to climb Mount Arafat, run to Hajar's well, and walk around the Jamarat, but he hunches his shoulders and walks the other way. The streets of Mecca carry him to dunes of people sitting under palm trees. He approaches coyly and sits next to a man from Palestine. He knows that the man is Palestinian from the way his dark eyes search for belonging. A thick-bearded imam named Muhammad stands on a rock lecturing about the gentleness of God. "He should be talking about hell," says the Palestinian man. "Hell is more believable than God."

He has Sartre's eyes and Moses's shyness. The cabin is warm, and the carrot-cake tray is empty. The guide introduces him as John. "He is known as the flower-man," she says. "No one in the Rockies knows native flora better than him." He blushes and wipes his round glasses. The American man is standing outside the window talking about him-related topics. Three excited girls sit at the front with pencils and notebooks. "I'm not as old as my hair wants you to believe," John begins with a joke, "but years of encountering grizzlies will suck the colour out of you." He divides the flowers of the Rockies into categories of colours and speaks about each flower the way Muhammad speaks of God's gentleness. He talks about blue harebell and violet alpine harebell and how both look the same to everyone but him, about rayflower and butterwort, which got their names from looking like a ray of light and having butter-coated petals, about *Saxifraga* flowers and mountain heathers, about *Nerium* shrubs, valerian roots, purple saw-wort, about the flowers that bears like best and the shrubs that elk like more, about which stem kills you and which makes you a cup of tea. He concludes with a picture of his wife and allows time for questions. I raise my hand and ask him if he could be a flower, which flower would he be. He blushes and avoids the answer. At night while using the drop, I hear a voice from behind the thin wall, "I'll be a heather. They look strong, but they fall at the slightest tremble."

He falls on his knees and weeps. Crowds of pilgrims push him back, but the scent of the Kaaba pulls him forward. The mountains I saw yesterday are no longer the same. I now know them by name. The saw-wort shimmers when I recognize its shade, and the heathers bow when I tread by them carefully. He skips a step to avoid trampling on a locust; spilled blood spoils pilgrimage. He runs under Ottoman arches, each arch a perfect reflection of the hundred before it. The rocks shake under my feet. God is waiting in the wet bush, on top of the mountain, by the black stone. The river flutters like the drapes of the Kaaba, and barefoot pilgrims bow like heathers. Aleph Lam Meem. My hands, an elk, a stream. Will God's image melt us like the people of Moses? Like jellyfish under the sun? We are our mothers' sons, always running towards God even when running away from him. John said that if two flowers of the same kind grow one inch apart, each flower will bloom with a different shade of colour depending on the soil. Was I rooted in dry land? Were you blooming in the light? We run past the arches and the mountains. He is there, nameless, waiting. We fall on our faces. Mother told us that everything revolves around God. Who knew she meant it literally? Planets and atoms and blood. We circle the Kaaba, the pines around the lake. You never knew such a shade of blue existed; I never knew a scent can be this sweet. A voice calls from behind the trees, an avalanche echoes from the minarets. We wash our faces in the lake, in Hajar's well, and the water stays clear.

CHAPTER II

FALL

Withhold no atom's atom,
or I die.

—JOHN KEATS

THE BODY

The larches are now golden. A colour that lasts for two weeks. In the Bow Valley, it is not uncommon for fall to be outlived by a fruit fly. By Moraine Lake, branches kneel to announce a passing, and tree trunks pearled with knots stand as if they know another way to wait. Today the world is dying, but I am only at the beginning of my life. Strapped pilgrims crowd the shores to crouch and ponder. What do they see? Klimt-yellow light limns the larch needles. The azure sky against their bright hue almost seems to be ebbing. A young woman, who arrived early, clicks her camera shutter over and over like a rosary, hungry for light, filled with light, and a Chinese man rocks against the wailing wind. What if death came to us like this, like autumn, like soft wind, like skin dissipating into a hundred pirouetting sand-coloured filaments, like so much beauty?

The larch season is a thin sheet of time that keeps winter from overlapping summer, and when it's pulled, a deluge of snow falls on the earth. On the earth, my body is folded in a blanket like origami. I came out here to lie, to watch, to be confused for grass. Winter

snaps something from me that I am yet to know. In
my chest there might be some deciduous bones. I hold
on with dear life before the wind pulls my sheet. I look
at my feet where the Chinese man sits, then I look up
at the sky, then back at my feet, but I lose the man,
or so I think. George B. Schaller writes that "during
transcendent experiences, such as during meditation,
brain activity is affected in that some neural traffic to
the cortex is shut down. As a result, the brain ceases
to make a distinction between self and the environment."[31] I wonder if that is what happened to the man.
If he, slowly, seeped into sedges. I try, too, to look at a
larch and confuse it with my hands, to squander my
blood like sap, but I can never succeed, or, rather, I
am afraid to. What if I, while seeping, sleep? Will I
wake up taller, full of beetles? Anyhow, who in their
right mind, after all those years of moulding, would
crumble for a balding larch. Yet I have found, mostly
in books, that effacement in the face of nature is not a
rare experience. Mary H. Kingsley, contemplating the
arrival of a beautiful African night, claimed that the
scene did not inspire in her "those complicated, poet-
ical reflections natural beauty seems to bring out in
other people's minds. It never works that way with me;
I just lose all sense of human individuality, all memory of human life, with its grief and worry and doubt,
and become part of the atmosphere."[32] John Muir
echoes this sentiment of self-forgetfulness: "Brooding

over some vast mountain landscape, or among the
spiritual countenances of mountain flowers, our bodies disappear, our mortal coils come off without any
shuffling, and we blend into the rest of Nature, utter-
ly blind to the boundaries that measure human quantities into separate individuals."[33] What about a bed
of flowers that makes us, without any shuffling, want
to sleep in it, to blend our bodies with its mud? Jean-
Jacques Rousseau's fictional character, Sainte-Preux,
attempts to answer the question while contemplating
the Alps: "In the end the spectacle has something – I
don't know what – of magic, of the supernatural, that
ravishes the spirits and the senses; one forgets everything, one forgets oneself, one no longer knows where
one is."[34] I am by Moraine Lake. I close my eyes and
count to three, but my hair doesn't evaporate, the tree
is still a tree. My hands, on the other hand, are turning red. The cold is losing itself. It is becoming me. The
"something" that Sainte-Preux found is somewhere
here, and it tests my edges, but I know now that sometimes to hold is to be held, and to let go is not to let
go of another but of a self that is held by another. It
is unfortunate that we cannot blink with our fingers
or hold things with our eyes. Nature either consumes
us whole, or not at all. And to fall on either camp one
must, apparently, choose between wisdom or sanity.
In the history of human immortality, those who tried
the nectar of forever were often touched by madness

and an absence of identity. It is almost as if endless living requires a ceasing of life, a letting go of everything.
The Jewish philosopher Martin Buber believed that
the "fleeting nature of actuality" and "the exalted mel-
ancholy of our fate" is caused by the fact that "every
Thou in our world must become an It."[35] To Buber, a
cat and a jar of cashews should not be gossiped about
as an "it" but as a "you/he/she." My table at home, the
tag on the back of my shirt, and the beetle by my feet
are all, supposedly, as much an "I" as any stubborn
baby who mumbles a self. The question, then, is how
does a coat hanger declare itself? To Buber, the answer
is a matter of perception. He considers an example
where he looks at a tree and sees it as "a picture: stiff
column in a shock of light," or as "movement: flow-
ing veins on clinging, pressing pith," or as numbers "in
pure numerical relation" or as "an expression of law"
that interacts with the laws around it. "In all this the
tree remains my object," Buber laments before he pro-
vides the remedy: "[The tree] can, however, also come
about, if I have both will and grace, that in considering
the tree I become bound up in relation to it. The tree
is now no longer It."[36] But to have will and grace is
not easy business. Buber is asking us of nothing more
than looking at a tree with love, and love, according to
Iris Murdoch, is the impossible "realization that something other than oneself is real."[37] That is why we disappear or become the atmosphere, because to hold the

plurality of nature is to let go of our individuality. To see my coat hanger as a subject, I have to tether the edges of the universe into hands other than mine. Carl Jung understood this well. He recalls a childhood experience where he almost lost himself to a stone:

> [T]here was a stone that jutted out – my stone. Often, when I was alone, I sat down on this stone, and then began an imaginary game that went something like this: "I am sitting on top of this stone and it is underneath." But the stone also could say "I" and think: "I am lying here on this slope and he is sitting on top of me." I would stand up, wondering who was what now. The answer remained totally unclear…The pull of that other world was so strong that I had to tear myself violently from the spot in order not to lose hold of my future.[38]

Jung had the will and the grace, but what he lacked was trust – trust that when letting go of the self he might, rather than lose it, find it in another. What Buber suggests is not an abandonment of selfhood but a realization of it outside of itself. The lover is not to forget that he is an I and that the tree is an It, but that they are neither and both at the same time; they are somewhere in the middle. They are, as he puts it, "confusedly entangled." This entanglement, before we learnt how to weave curtains, was a covenant: "For

thou shalt be in league with the stones of the field:
and the beasts of the field shall be at peace with thee."[39]
This entanglement was the only way to live, to be in
the world, but it came at a cost. To be one with nature
is to be no one at all.

***

In Istanbul, I visited a Sama ceremony to take pictures
of the whirling dervishes, and, after a few chants, I saw
the hems of their dresses turning a transparent char-
treuse. In their trance, they were transcending – out of
themselves and into themselves. The little booklet in
my hands explained that dervishes dance until their
dizziness makes them forget their edges. Only then
can the limitless divine pour into the limits of their
bodies like water over water. The prefix "trans" comes
from the Latin *tere*, to move through, over, across, or
beyond. To be transfixed is to be rendered motionless
by a movement outside of you that moves through you,
for a feeling to be translated, or carried across, to you.
Sailors, after returning from sea, adjust their steps to
match the stillness of the ground. Their eyes watch the
waves for so long that their bodies transpose into a careening. After the Sama, after seeing the dervishes, I
won't swear for you to believe me, I had to touch my
cheeks, to lean on a wall, to relearn my dimensions.

***

Here, the larches spin to some nameless wind, and I've been watching for some time. It is not mystery that the observer wants, nor a parable, but a forgiveness attained only through dissolving, a knowledge gained only through forgetfulness. Will I see my hands in a larch the way I see my face in every lake? Who knows. Man, according to Christopher Manes, is "the self-proclaimed soliloquist of the world."[40] Are the larches only a creation of their pilgrims' own image? I roll around the grass until my elbows are muddied. The young woman and the Chinese man, standing still like prairie dogs, are rolling too. The brush of the breeze, my dry hair, the swaying trunk, the swirling clouds, the shoulder of the hill, the gullies in my ribs. We're all spinning – spinning out of our edges. I am not my flesh, but my body is not turning green. I am only transient, rolling over, across, beyond, in between. And when I begin to feel the pull, I let go of some of me, then I tear myself from the ground like wet clay.

If what I was told is true; that if I think, then I am, then not to think is to be anything that I can. If the head is spun into transparency, the body can transition into a membrane, a melody.

The Chinese man is now resting against a boulder. He gives me a polite nod. There is dirt under his nails. There is so much colour under the sky. I want it under my nails, but such desires come with a feeling

of shame. To want the world as a thing rather than
an idea is fanatical, but the foot of the mountain, the
head of the valley, the arm of the creek, and, as Gretel
Ehrlich found, "the waist of the arctic"[41] are all words
that ask us to think of land as a metaphor. What does
it mean that this body of earth, from the foot of any
pine to the shores of Minnewanka, is a body, while the
space between my toes and forehead is also a body?
On my mouth there is longing, and on the mouth of
Moraine is hesitancy. Neither of us can carry across
what we really mean. Spruce tied and cold, we wait
and quiver.

Schaller notes that, to Tibetan Buddhists, walking
across the Pemako landscape is like moving through
the body of the female deity Vajrayogini. Only a saun-
tering pilgrim can know the mystery of her form. Each
part of the land represents a part of the deity, "Gyala
Peri symbolizes her head, Namcha Barwa and Kangla
Karpo her breasts, the Doxiong La her hips, and the
Rinchenpung temple her navel."[42] When language
transitions an object into a metaphor, it transforms
its meaning and blurs its definition. Linguistically
speaking, there is an interesting overlap between lips,
hills, and the word "palilalia," as all three belong to
a body (a body of an animal, a body of land, a body
of text). The body, then, becomes a thing to be read,
loved, exploited, devoured, dissected, killed, etcetera.
Metaphors confuse our associations of signs that we

mistake a poem for a plum and a patch of grass for a psalm. "What is a farm but a mute gospel," exclaimed a jubilant Emerson.[43] Metaphors turn our thoughts into food and grow apples in our eyes. To the Greeks, Atlas was both a mountain and a man, "beard and hair were forests and his arms and shoulders / Were mountain ridges; what had been his head / Was the peak of the mountain, and his bones were boulders."[44] Even these mountains that we now call the Rockies were called, by their original people, "Backbone-of-the-world."[45] And since the land gives us food, bodies incite desire, and texts feed us knowledge, fruits and sex and letters become interchangeable. The etymologist Mark Forsyth joked, "Freud said that everything was secretly sexual, but etymologists know that sex is secretly food."[46] In his book *Pleasures of the Text* Roland Barthes argues that texts seduce and wound, they desire and demand. To Barthes, the textual is sexual. Alberto Manguel affirms this by noting that the "fear of what a reader might do among the pages of the book is like the ageless fear men have of what women might do in the secret places of their body,"[47] and Ezequiel Martínez Estrada claims that recalling previous texts while reading is "one of the most delicate forms of adultery."[48] There is a level of perversion in unveiling a body of text from between its covers and gazing at it without any sense of hesitation. It is reported that Muslims blush and tremble when they open the Quran and then kiss its covers when they are done reading it. The confusion of symbols is intensified when considering that, in the Arabic language, the word for literature, cultivation, and feasting is the same: *adab*. In a famous incident, a seventh-century Arab woman named Hind ate the heart of a man out of anger. Similarly, a missionary named David Wood ate pages of the Quran out of spite, while in Tehran, Salman Rushdie's books were burnt like the flesh of a Salem witch. Such events can hardly be called rare. In the Torah, Jeremiah assures God, "When your words came, I ate them,"[49] and Benjamin Alire Sáenz writes in his poem "To The Desert," "Break me, I am bread."[50] Tribes in Papua New Guinea consume the brains of their ancestors to inherit their spirits, and Christians practise cannibalism on a weekly basis: "Take, eat; this is my body. And he took the cup, and gave thanks, and gave it to them, saying, Drink ye all of it; For this is my blood."[51] Even stranger is the fact that most of our food comes from the earth, and most creation myths affirm that we, whether from corn or from clay, came from earth too. Sylix theorist Jeannette Armstrong writes, "In our language, the word for our bodies contains the word for land…in my mind, every time I say that word and I refer to myself, I realize that I am from the land. I'm saying that I'm from the land and that my body is the land."[52] Heart and pomegranate and paragraphs are all to be tasted, all to be read like a hand. Babies have a habit of snatching any alien object they find on the ground and then hurling it into their mouths. They know the world through eating it. The act of consuming is nothing more than a desire to merge, to bend boundaries, to collapse the distinction between subject and object, or, if one is hungry enough, between subject and subject. That is perhaps why Eve ate the apple, because its name wasn't enough.

Consider geophagy, an eating disorder that encourages an appetite for eating earth. In some regions, however, earth is craved culturally, rather than medically. Clay bars are sold in Ugandan markets the way Hershey bars are sold in Canadian stores. The practice can also be found in Thailand, Turkey, and rural Alabama. Geophagists, contrary to common belief, do not just crudely eat any pile of dirt. They have a refined taste for "hardened clay of a termite nest" or "the soft, white soil in a particular riverbank."[53] This type of eating disorder is known as pica, a term derived from the Latin name for the magpie, *Pica pica* (a bird who is rumoured to have a diet consisting of anything under the sun). The focus of pica can vary from an appetite for hair (trichophagia), feces (coprophagia), stones (lithophagia), wood (lignophagia), and, painfully, sharp objects (acuphagia). A medical paper reports a 6-year-old African girl who was brought to a clinic after her father admitted her for "eating the textbooks at school." When the doctor asked her why

she ate the books, the girl replied, "I don't know." [54] I
have exhausted the niche, isolated shelf on psychiatry
in the library and found no mention of a book-eating
pica. The peculiar diet is, unfortunately, always mis-
taken for xylophagia – paper eating. But the nameless
African girl, as some other scattered cases, reported
only eating books and not paper of all kinds. It is then
unjust to confuse the cravings. Eating apples as opposed to apple trees is a very different practice. The
term bibliophagy, book eating, is always defined as a
figurative devouring, as a voracious act of reading, but
I do not believe the term to be symbolic, or the disorder to be medical. It is semantic at heart. The African
girl suffers from nothing more than a literal understanding of Francis Bacon's claim, "some books are to
be tasted, others to be swallowed, and some few to be
chewed and digested." [55]

On the surface of Lake Moraine, light pops like
corn kernels, and the needles of the larches fall like
so much honey. Thoreau claimed once that he wanted "to suck out all the marrow of life." [56] Last year, following a map to Skoki Lodge near Lake Louise, I was
directed to take a left at the fork. To my surprise, there
was a two-metre-long wooden fork jammed into the
earth. What if I had pulled it? What if I twisted it and
gathered the bluebells around its fingers like fettuc-
cine? I walk around the larches and an urge fills my
mouth to pluck this smoked-mustard September like

a pear. I don't want to become the atmosphere; my
shoulders are not broad enough to circle all this air.
Borges claims that few writers succeed in becoming
immortalized in things: "The moon, springtime, the
nightingales all manifest the glory of Heinrich Heine,"
while the "long railway platforms and docks, Walt
Whitman." He then celebrates that "the best immor-
talities" are still waiting for someone to become them.
"There is no poet who is the total voice of love, hate, or
despair."[57] If only I can be this hair-thin golden needle
falling on the shore of this moraine, I will gladly give
up the little sanity I have in me. For now, all I have
is the confusion, but soon, perhaps, the entanglement
will follow. The grace. The will. The peace.

CHAPTER III

WINTER

Beauty is nothing but the
beginning of terror.

—RAINER MARIA RILKE

FATHER TO THE MAN

I woke up yesterday and found a hole in my sock. The hole, of course, happened without my awareness, without my consent. The fray between flesh and fibre was silent, like a blizzard at night. I woke up and the world was suddenly not what I closed my eyes to. I looked out my window and shuddered. Are we ever safe? Normally, this would not have been a matter of concern, but for the last few nights, I have spent my sight's last light on the prophets of the Jews, the treatise of al-Ghazali, and an anthology of English sonnets. An amalgamation of texts that appears innocent until a sock gets ripped.

By the window, the prying daylight demanded decisions. What an anxious life it is when a metaphor is forced on you before a cup of coffee. I held the sock like a letter and tried to understand it. I had three options. One, close the hole, as St. Paul would. Heal it before it festers. Two, ignore it, until the entire sole finds its way out of what was thought to be an insignificant hole. Three, and most probable, throw it away and forget about the mishap, forget about the cues, like the Jews in the desert. Be the koan: the man who woke up

every day without a sock and went to bed asking God
for warmth. There is, of course, a fourth option, but
that one is for the mad.

Two weeks ago, at exactly 11:26 p.m., the first snow-
flake of winter made contact with the ground. The first
snow fell like hesitant hatchlings, and now it lands on
anything, anywhere. Each storm passes us with the
same question we ask of interstate ice cream shops:
What are you doing here? I have no answer, but I am
glad the rain is over. As a child, I thought rain was
God's way of sending us urgent messages, and that
people who carried umbrellas were as rude as devils. I
would stretch my hand and read the drops of rain for
Morse code, or I would listen to the neighbour's tin
roof for clues. With heavy rain God always sènt the
letter *H*, so I would laugh until I fell asleep. Drizzles,
on the other hand, brought meaning as strange as
Revelation, asking me to dig, or, sometimes, to hide.
I quit the habit of listening after a night when the tin
roof was hysterically rattling $\cdots - - - \cdots$. God was
sending the universal signal for distress, S.O.S.

In the winter, there is nothing to do but walk around
and look at how the world changed. I walk up Muskrat
Street and I think, *there used to be a bench where that
snow is*. Then I make my way to the canoe docks and
observe, *there used to be docks where that snow is*.
And so on, until I know all that has been swallowed.
That's all I do. Everyday, I go out of my room to look at

things, but, day by day, there is barely anything left to see. The same Engelmann spruces, slanting. The same piles of snow, growing. The same blotches of sky, dissipating. I notice some new tracks over a hill; I yawn. When I first moved here, the sight of my breath playing with the October air thrilled me. Now, forests are dying; I sit in bed eating scrambled eggs. I am uncertain whether to diagnose myself with age or habit. I find that once you reach a certain age, an absence of experience becomes the only welcomed experience. Perhaps that's how we prepare ourselves for death. Tolstoy writes, "if the whole complex lives of many people go on unconsciously, then such lives are as if they had never been."[58] It is much more comforting to slip into the unconscious, to stay in the cave, to not question or be questioned by noise, but I hate to be a waste of cosmic ashes. I don't want a star to sigh, *is this what we burst for?* So I leave my bed and, for the star's sake, I go out to seek. I look at elk and I try to see them. I look at evergreens and I try to see them. I look at rocks and I try to see them, but I rarely succeed. Seeing is impossibly difficult. The moment I *see* a rock I am distracted from it by it. Viktor Shklovsky writes, "if we start to examine the general laws of perception, we see that as perception becomes habitual, it becomes automatic."[59] This automation of perception is to prevent our brain wires from overheating. The automation allows us to look and move on. Otherwise,

a single gaze would take days. When I look out my
window, I do not see the trees, I recognize them. My
brain brushes them off. *You know it's a tree*, it tells me,
but look, what is that yellow thing? Habit is the other
sleep; without it, life would become tiring, but with it,
it becomes transient. One must choose, and I, abetted
by astronomical ablation, choose to see. To do so, I
must see like an artist, at least that's what Shklovsky
prescribes, "art exists that one may recover the sensation of life."[60] He recommends this be done through
two methods: by prolonging the activity of perception
and by the defamiliarization of the object. He promises that this remedy will make "the stone stony."

I make a cup of oolong and sit by my window attempting the first method of seeing; I look at a tree
for hours. But the tree has multiple branches, and
each branch has twigs, and each twig has needles, etcetera. Who knew? It's maddening. I try to settle on
one branch, but a squirrel comes and steals my seeing.
Thank the squirrel. The oolong is now turning bitter,
so I push it aside, next to my holed sock, into a corner
of all the things I don't want to see.

I take my bike out to the snow-covered golf course
loop along the Spray River. I speed down the hill in a
thrill. I am on the hunt for everything.

I sit on some wet grass by the river. To tune my seeing, I pick up an aspen leaf that has been topograph-
ized by a leaf miner. How does one defamiliarize a

leaf? How do I unleaf it? And even if I do, won't that, paradoxically, make it leafy? Muslims warn not to make *a'da* from *i'bada*, not to allow the act of praying to become an act of habit. A Sufi teacher preaches:

> When looking at a bowl we only perceive it, but we do not understand it. The meaning of a bowl is learnt through use rather than observation, but once the bowl is learnt, it no longer becomes a thing to be discovered or, subsequently, a thing to be seen. It is the novice's greatest error to hold as a fact a meaning which is habitually inferred. The task of the pursuer of truth, then, is to baptize oneself from habit; to look at things as innocently as a child; to see every object as new, undiscovered, uncategorized.[61]

If seeing is an act of forgetting, then seeing is terrifying. The sky above me is mottled with pine needles. What if I forget what a leaf is and then look up? Would I think the heavens are cracking?

I study the mines in the leaf. There is no methodology to the leaf miner except chaos. It eats its way in any direction possible, and who's to blame it? If I was born in a tiramisu, I would not strategize. I would open my mouth and run. I look at the leaf, the browning petiole, the tip, the half-munched veins. The leaf miner ate God, the devil, and the detail. The venules are tangled like a bad metaphor, like thunder under a line of clouds. The lamina is limpidly delineated like a caustic ocean, while the midrib splits the surface. I squint further, and I see the green of the green, the gap in the seam, but some fear jolts me to scale out and look away. When I do, the light is bright and blinding. My eyes see nothing but blotches of shamrock. My head spins. The world swallows me. Was it always this wide? Emerson once remarked that to paint a tree one must become a tree. To see like an artist is to become what you see. I close my eyes and crumble the leaf in my hand to remind myself that I am bigger than leaf miner and lamina. I open my eyes to the river, and I *see* it! It slithers in threads of black and white and blue. Who knew? It spreads like a sheet of a reeling Pollock, repeating its patterns again and again. I look at the river, no longer noticing the green of the grass under or the trees across. It is as if I have never known a colour other than that of the river. I tether my eyes to its fibre, I anchor my sight in its quiver, and if not for the cold that pokes my bones, I would have never realized that I am standing knee-deep in its confused current. There is so much to see now. There, a sparrow midair. Sun, berries, air! I stumble out of the river in baptism. Hosanna. The branches bend. Under them there is grass, so I fall on my knees to pray. If there was a God who made this earth, he must have been a child. The first thing a child says after witnessing magic is *do it again*, while only the habituated adults ask *how?*

God pulled a thread of grass and couldn't believe it, so he said again, and then again, and again, and again, and again, and again, and again. He then came out of his exuberance and saw that he had made a meadow, and, again, he couldn't believe it. "The child," writes Wordsworth, "is father of the man."[62]

The loop, which normally takes 20 minutes of lazy paddling, took me four hours to complete. I stop to see everything. A family of cyclists pass me. Who are we to not be stopped by a bush when Yahweh was. I fear to be smitten by thunder, again and again and again, so I stop, and I push my face in the bush. Seeing is a process of dismantling. You cannot see the world from afar. You must get close. You must shove your being in it. al-Hallaj complains to God in his poem, "you drew me so close to you that I forgot who was who."[63] Is that what Shklovsky meant when he wrote that seeing is a plurality of being?

I return to my room and grab a yellow thread to sew my sock, again and again. This is why my mother never bothered with rosaries. I don't conceal the hole. Like the Japanese, I mark it with gold. The Sufis were right, and Paul was not mad after all. I wear the sock and I run to the meadows; "for my power is made perfect in weakness...for when I am weak, then I am strong."[64]

HEAVINESS

Saturday:

The moon is halfway to Latvia. Its beam undulates through my window like water, almost tangible, and coruscates like chrome wind chimes, almost audible. Half asleep, I stretch my hand to ladle the light, and the moon pours, overflows, floods. When I was a child, the moon was a metre closer, now it swims away at a rate of four centimetres per year – the same growth rate of a human child, but what shelf is the moon trying to reach? It is a strange thing to wake up in the middle of a sleep and think of silk, or the abnormally large antennae of male cerambycid beetles, or of anything other than sleep. Do our brains talk to themselves the way we do? Do I glimpse a part of it that I am not supposed to know by waking up without knocking? Tonight, I was pulled out of a sleep with the sound of a word ringing in my brain. By the light of my lamp, I do not know what the word means or in what language it was, but in my dream, not only did I understand it, but I knew it the way I know the taste

of my mouth. Who am I to myself? I must know before breakfast.

Outside, the mountains are headless. Clouds gnaw
on Cascade Mountain's shoulders like swarms of
Mormon crickets, and they continue their descent
swallowing the mountain whole, "and they shall cover
the face of the earth, that one shall not be able to see
the earth."[65]

I pray for seagulls.

It is cold, so cold that my neighbour called a day of
-16°C weather warm. The winter empties the streets. I
walk to the blue houses at the end of Squirrel Street
and then walk back. I walk because if I stay in any
longer, I might turn into a rug. My room smells like
forgotten cups of tea. I force myself into daily rituals
to keep me from straying. Saturdays are for emptying.
I write. I play the piano. I yell. Of course, rituals do
not always deliver what they intend. Anne Fadiman,
in her book *Ex Libris*, reports that "Kipling was incapable of writing fiction with a pencil," and that Virginia
Woolf complained, "what am I going to say with a de-
fective nib?"[66] I blame my creaking chair.

Sunday:

I read all day. I read about dirt, the etymology of fruit
names, and baby language. I also read instruction
handbooks. If the miracle of nature is in its details,
then car manuals should be sacred. It is hard to believe

that someone sat down and wrote them into existence; the anatomy of a car's key, the function of the cylinder head, the sensation of wind buffeting, which is described as "the perception of pressure on the ears or a helicopter-type sound."[67] There are exactly 127,731 words in the manual I'm reading, and there are 77,430 words in the Quran. 127,731 words to describe a few metal sheets and windshield wipers, and almost half of that to describe the whole world, the after world, the seen, the unseen, and what's in between.

When I am tired of detail, I read things that lack it. I read about the early mountaineers who came here, mountaineers who often found these mountains impossible to explain – a strange problem since mountains are the only subject of a mountaineers' writing. Take James Thorington, one of the earliest explorers of the Canadian Rockies, who, upon seeing a sunset at the Icefields, uttered what are perhaps the most common phrases used in mountaineering literature, "beyond all words," "no description does justice," "you should be there yourself to understand."[68] He writes later, discussing the mountains he encountered, "they can never mean to the reader quite what they mean to those who took part of them. You must go yourself to comprehend."[69] James Outram, another legendary pioneer in the Rockies, wrote helplessly when seeing Lake Louise, "words fail to conjure up the glories."[70] While Morley Roberts, returning from his trip to the park, denied the mountains all together; "They were not real. I, or someone else, had imagined them."[71] Terrain was not the only thing early mountaineers had to discover. They also had to find a language for that terrain. But the issue does not seem restricted to this region. Across cultures and histories, we find that people were often incapable of speaking about mountains, an ineffability similar to the one mystics have of the divine. In the seventh century CE, a well-known poem from the *Manyōshū*, the oldest known anthology of Japanese poetry, describes Mount Fuji as such: "It baffles the tongue, it cannot be named / It is a god mysterious."[72] And in the Puranas, ancient works of Hindu mythology, the religious text is only capable to describe the Himalayas as indescribable: "I could not describe to you the glories of Himachal."[73] The Japanese critic Sanari Kentaro explains that "the reason why there are curiously few fine poems in Japanese or Chinese, or fine paintings about Fuji, is that the subject is too overpoweringly splendid."[74] Similarly, God is often seen in the same terms. Pope Francis, echoing Thorington's claim that "you must be there to understand," preached in a sermon that "God is a mystery that cannot be understood, but only encountered and lived."[75] And just as Du Fu wrote, "With what can I compare the Great Peak [of Mount Tai]?"[76] the Quran tells us "there is nothing comparable to [God]."[77] But why mountains? Why not oceans or deserts? Almost every single major religion began on top of some mountain. Moses received his commandments on Mount Sinai; Jesus delivered his sermon on a mountain and overcame the devil on another; Muhammad was spoken to on Mount Hira; the Greeks built an abode or their gods on Mount Olympus; Odin dwells on a high hill called Hliðskjálf; Buddhists know the Himalayas as the home of their gods; and the Stoney People of the Bow Valley seek the peaks for divine visions. I now wonder, have flat lands ever inspired any revelation? One answer, perhaps, is that mountains are the meeting places between mortals and gods. We ascend, and they descend. Mountains, unlike meadows and rivers, force us to look up – a practice we reserve for praying.

The difficulty of talking about mountains, however, is not only of ineptitude. Mountains invite a language that cannot escape being gaudy when depicting the epic. John Muir was often criticized because "all his mountain streams sang psalms," because of his "happy birds" and "glad brooks" and "joyous wildflowers," but, mostly, he is faulted for his excessive use of the word "glorious." Muir himself was aware of this. He wrote to a friend once that he spends his days "slaughtering 'glorious' in his manuscript."[78] The issue is augmented when considering that most literary figures of the 20th century preferred being thought heartless than sincere. Read, for example, Bukowski's "There's a bluebird in my heart that wants to get out, but I pour whiskey on him."[79] Or Oscar Wilde's claim that "all bad poetry springs from genuine feeling."[80] Or Keith Waldrop's declaration that "a bad poem is always sincere."[81] I pity the mountaineer; after a day of pushing against gravity and gravel, over pinnacle and precipice, proud, pleased, fulfilled, fails to push the limits of a language that can be entirely gathered in a dictionary lighter than a shoe and settles for writing, "If you glimpse but a bit of it, great indeed will be our reward."[82] Rundle Mountain is in view. Geologically, it is a "writing-desk," rock that has been "tilted 20–40 degrees during the horizontal compression of mountain pile-up."[83] Geographically, a pile of limestone and shale positioned at 51°07'27"N and 115°28'13"W. Historically, a name given after the Methodist missionary Reverend Robert Rundle. Recreationally, a moderately challenging trail that takes around eight to ten hours to complete. Intimately, an unsayable presence, a warm familiarity, a shoulder, a home. You can walk, climb, break, take, pierce, and summit an earth, but water carries you where it wants.

I pray for glimpses.

Monday:

Mondays are for mending; I glue the chair. I do the laundry. I trim my hair. I pluck out all the wilting leaves from my plants, all the mould out of old

teacups, all the hope twisting my eyes, and then I toss
them, wash them, or hold on to them. Mondays I sit
where there's sun. I follow the rays around the house
like a leaf. I sit by my window. I lie where the door
lets in a light thinner than my nose. In the winter, a
warm sunray is a delicacy, and like all the things of
the dirt I creep to it. I sit to think of why I sit, why I
think. I bring my palms side by side and look at them.
The line going across them forms a bowl. What am I
to learn from dust filling it? I like to think that there
is depth to my thinking, but there's only a sound like
a cat purring. Alone, the minutes, like honeycrisps,
peel against my fingers and hushed mice feet dance
around my silence like smoke signals saying *this is the
bridge bending.* Alone, I see the present naked like a
rock chipped by chinook. God might have misunder-
stood man when he decreed it "not good for man to
be alone."[84] Every year we increase at a rate of 1.1 per
cent. Every year loneliness recedes at a rate of 1.1 per
cent. Nowadays, it is so very difficult to sit around and
do nothing. Nothingness, like the black rhino, is dying.
Sometimes I want like a butterfly to believe my skin, to
trust that if I lie still under all the gaping noise, no one
will see me. From the edge of my house, snow peeks
at the emptiness inside. The winter is dark, but in the
world there's too much light. There's a billion empty
stars. It's not one question to think about. It's a billion
questions to consider. If only one mosquito remained

on Earth, what would we think of our hands? Recently, I've felt as if life had a god who suddenly died, and everything now is without substance, without marrow. All the green is now grey, yet, strangely, I find the grey more beautiful, the hollowness tight enough to occlude me from seeping. I keep the snow at bay.

I pray for nothing.

Tuesday:

I play a game of Scrabble with my neighbour, Nicole. The random letters in front of me remind me of the old question, if a monkey sat by a typewriter for an infinite amount of time, would it be able to produce Shakespeare's *Hamlet*? I think the question is redundant, because it neglects to consider if the monkey has the will to write at all. I came here for tea, I had no intention of writing even a hello, but Nicole insists, and this monkey has no will. From playing, I learn that the letters for *listen* make *silent* too. I place a heart right through her breath, and she dangles a whale on my waist. In Scrabble, each letter is assigned a value, a weight. The more common the letter, the less value it has. "Hello" and "grief" are heavier than "iron." On a square white paper, Nicole had written all the words that can be made from two letters and their meanings. Starting from KU and ending at OD, the lines read as follows:

A Māori digging stick

Cows
A musical note
A Chinese distance unit
Look, behold
Mother
Myself
A musical note
Sound of satisfaction
A moment
A Greek letter
Belonging to me
A Greek letter
To approach
An objection
A mystical universal force

I lose the game by 60 points. Sixty points I couldn't bear the weight of. I only had the will to place two letters at a time, but it doesn't matter what the monkey types, or in what order. Look, behold, there will be cows, a moment, a musical note, half my family, and a mystical universal force.

Wednesday:

Somewhere there must be a place where the snow is born, but like my waking thoughts I can never find it. Here, we are at most only an hour of its life. I sit outside by a tree watching the clouds pass. In an open field, a person will always lie by a tree, a bush, a rock.

It's within us to mistrust space. There's barely a flake of snow between the twig and its sister, barely any air, and my toes chafe one another, ache with blisters, but out there, just above the cluttered cluster, the jeering ether stretches still. There is not enough light here for me to measure it. Emptiness that can fit galaxies but not fill a balloon. The world is expanding, but I can barely find a parking spot. In the valley under these clouds, there are so many trees. What weight would they be assigned? And what about all the human heads, small and scattered like pollen? Are we losing our value at a rate of 1.1 per cent per year? There is so much beauty in the valley, but why can't I say the same about all the streets that interrupt the mountains? Naturalists have been asking the same question for years: If beaver dams and mink scat are natural, then why aren't our skyscrapers and two-dollar frozen pizzas? Are we part of nature or apart from it?

Behind my window, I watch the snow melt on the glass, but outside, my feet get cold. The answer might entirely depend on where we stand. That's why ecologists and theologians share the same problem; after all the studies and observations, all the hermeneutics and theories, all the equations and devotion, the environmentalist will tell you what any Bedouin knew for generations: "don't be greedy." Because the answer to our problem is not to know, but to be, and that is why avid hikers and zealous Taoists are indistinguishable.

According to Alan Levinovitz, Nature is just another word for God, and according to Raymond Williams, Nature is the most complex word in the English language. Since the Enlightenment, we've been trying to pull the curtains to unveil an answer. What is Nature? But if a man's intentions can be worked out from what he spends most of his attention on, then the answer to Nature's question can easily be summed in one word: beetles. Christopher Manes claims that "evolution has no goal, or if it does we cannot discern it, and at the very least it does not seem to be us. The most that can be said is that during the last 350 million years natural selection has shown an inordinate fondness for beetles."[85] In his article, "An Inordinate Fondness for Beetles," David Quammen recounts the famous story of a theologian asking the geneticist J.B.S. Haldane "what inferences one could draw, from a study of the created world, as to the nature of its creator." To which Haldane responded, "an inordinate fondness for beetles."[86] And in the book, *An Inordinate Fondness for Beetles*, the authors claim that "if single examples of every plant and animal species were placed in a row, every fifth species would be a beetle."[87] There are more species of beetles than names of God, more beetles on Earth than words. There is a beetle for every colour, for every species of tree, for every region of Earth. It is not one thing to consider, but a billion things to consider. Edward O. Wilson was wise enough to state that the number of beetles is one of those questions that we simply can never know the answer to. Maybe nature is like that too. Maybe that's what Yeats meant when he wrote, "Man can embody truth but he cannot know it."[88] Maybe I should go outside and feel the cold in the bones of my feet. Maybe that's the closest to truth I'll ever be. Maybe.

Sometimes I think that if the world followed the rules of Scrabble, then all the beetles, all the sand in the Sahara, all the pines in the Bow Valley, and all our fingers would weigh less than a piping bird. We have always dreamt of infinite time, but if I look up at the infinite space above me, I find it empty, endless, meaningless, and I am barely a pip of it. There is never enough time in space, and never enough space in time. The world is large and the days are laced. If I stretch a foot, I'll tumble tomorrow. To be always here and never here seems to be one and the same thing. Sometimes when the sun seeps through my sleep and sweeps me into the living, lurching tall woods where things like mayflies and spiders live a tree apart, I think that perhaps the intention of the sky is not to make us feel small but only to make us feel smaller. It gives me joy to know that a cloud, no matter how pressed, will not answer me. This od, this mystical universal force that begins with gold and ends with nothing, repeats itself every day, and we run out to solve it, we run to know it, and although the creek might carry clues and the hills hint to some answer, they will never shout it at you, because who wants to believe in life the way they believe in gravity. We want to fall and not know whether there's hope or hell. That's the thrill. George Steiner wrote in 1991 that "it has been estimated that since the late 1780s, some 25,000 books, essays, articles, contributions to critical and learned colloquia, doctoral dissertations, have been produced on the true meaning of *Hamlet*."[89] Whether it is Shakespeare or a monkey who is patting down their thoughts does not matter one bit, because whatever is written will always be a mystery, because "though this be madness, yet there is method in't."[90]

I pray for uncertainties.

Thursday:

Thursdays I go to the Canmore Crossway Community Thrift. An odd little place nestled between mountains and train tracks. In there, you'll find North Face cargo pants and Columbia sweaters for $10 a piece, but an Arabic darbuka will cost you around $100. I leave the place with a piebald pistachio ceramic teapot ($5), pristine beige socks dappled with achromic anchors ($3), an *Encyclopedia of Vanished Species* with a parrot on the cover that I swear I saw somewhere in a zoo ($3), and an Olympia typewriter that was blasphemously labelled as a "printer" ($10). The typewriter is now in front of me. It sits without a cover, and its skeleton lies bare on the wooden desk. The ribbon spool is coiling a fresh, vivid black belt, the typebars glisten with nascent dexterity, and the carriage lever protrudes like a hand expecting a kiss. By the bold Olympia decal, another two labels dot the machine: a red circular sticker with the promise "TESTED," and a bisque laminated note marked with a dying declaration, "Property of Leo. C: 12B. 1962." I roll a paper into the platen and secure its margins. It is time to test its TESTED label. I press V and a hand jolts from inside the machine slapping a quick rising Mylar ribbon like a guaranteed whack-a-mole win. The ribbon goes down leaving a V perfectly stamped into the paper. Every key is accompanied with a ring and ink. The music is both heard and seen. When I told the cashier that I wanted the typewriter, she slanted her eyebrows, "have you tried carrying it?" The machine, equipped with a foot-long, cold-rolled, steel-cylinder platen, weighs around 30 pounds – an adult elephant's heart. I had to ask for a ride home.

**

In 1881, a myopic Nietzsche, who complained that 20 minutes of reading or writing made him feel pain, bought a Malling-Hansen writing ball, a typing machine that resembles a medieval torture device, to aid him in writing without having to depend entirely on his vision. He enjoyed the machine so much that he dedicated a poem to it:

> The writing ball is a thing like me: made of iron
> Yet easily twisted on journeys.
> Patience and tact are required in abundance
> As well as fine fingers to use us.

After a while, Nietzsche noticed something odd. He sent a letter to a friend professing that "our writing tools are also working on our thoughts."[91] The philosopher felt that his thoughts were changing due to the change of the process of writing them, making things like "long sentences not much of an option." In his book, *Gramophone, Film, Typewriter*, the German scholar, Friedrich A. Kittler, compares Nietzsche's writing prior to and after the purchase of the writing ball and finds that Nietzsche's prose "changed from arguments to aphorisms, from thoughts to puns, from rhetoric to telegram style." He then concludes: "Malling Hansen's writing ball, with its operating difficulties, made Nietzsche into a laconic."[92] Nietzsche was not alone with suspecting the innocence of a typewriter. Martin Heidegger, perhaps a little dramatically, declares the typewriter as "a signless cloud, i.e., a withdrawing concealment in the midst of its very obtrusiveness."[93] He continues, now a little biblically, "the hand sprang forth only out of the word and together with the word," and the typewriter is to blame for tearing "writing from the essential realm of the hand, i.e., the realm of the word." He goes on, now with the tone of a galled juvenile; "The typewriter makes everyone look the same." I wanted to know for myself if there is a difference between the written and the typed, and the level, if any, of a medium's intrusion on the message. Do typewriters, like cursed dolls, feign innocence as they sit motionless on our shelves while secretly plotting the complete "destruction of the word"?[94]

I began writing, but I stopped at the first word. Unlike the silent birth of an inked letter, the typed letter is born screaming, and it's impossible to escape the consequences of giving it life; it declares it to the highest sky. You press an *O*, and a thud is pressed back at you. You continue, quickly, frightened, with an *N*, *C*, *E*, but the sounds don't fade into one another, you feel them individually, like a trinity, each holding its own weight, and even when the word is completed, it clings and rings in your head like a gong. I stop, not out of fear of becoming laconic but because by the end of the first paragraph my neighbours were knocking on my wall.

I want to propose, if what I say has any weight at all, that writing should not be a silent practice; it should, like Scrabble letters, carry weight. No one in their right mind, claimed Paul de Man, would try to grow grapes by the light of the word "day." But we used to. "If the righteous wished to create a world," the Talmud tells us, "they could do so."[95] We used to move the world by moving our tongues. We used to write gods into life, but now if I write the mountains on fire, the grass outside will still be wet. Writing doesn't smell, doesn't move, doesn't unclog a sink. Writing, at its best, is a festoon, a red balloon, a chandelier, but never a home. What happened? An early Sumerian poem speaks of the genesis of writing as such, "The messenger's mouth was heavy, he couldn't repeat the message. The Lord of Kulab patted some clay, he put the words on it."[96] This is how it began, out of a necessary heaviness, not the dear diary mundanity, not cheap neon signs, not labels and tags and manuals. Fadiman tells the story of Sir Walter Scott, who, while hunting, perfected "a sentence he had been trying to compose all morning… Before it could fade, he shot a crow, plucked a feather, sharpened the tip, dipped it in crow blood, and captured the sentence."[97] The most I can do for a sentence is to get out of bed for it. The Chinese Chiaku-wen writers deposited their words on tortoise shells and ox scapula. In the ancient world, most things were written on animal hide and stone tablets. If writing a thought into a typewriter is inconvenient, imagine slaughtering a camel for it, pressing it on a rock, writing it in blood. Imagine the noise, the screaming, the trouble. What sort of heaviness pressed them to do so? When the angel Gabriel came to Muhammad

and ordered him to "read," the prophet protested, "I
don't know how to read." Three times the angel repeated the command, "read," until the prophet ran
in fear and contemplated throwing himself from on
top of the Meccan mountains. The frightened prophet rushed home, trembling, "*zamilooni, dathirooni.*"
Cover me, wrap me. But God ordered him to stand,
"For we shall charge thee with a word of weight."[98] It
was a word of weight that Moses in Exodus implores
not to carry: "Pardon your servant, Lord. Please send
someone else."[99] It was a word of weight that knocked
Paul from his donkey, crushed Omar al-Khattab and
made him throw his sword, pushed Constantine to
march with an army, made Jeremiah forget language
"Ah, Lord Yahweh, look, I do not know how to speak.
I am a child."[100] It was a word of weight that came to
a fig tree where St. Augustine was weeping and whispered what the angel asked of the prophet, "*tolle,
lege.*" Take up and read. It was a word of weight that
ordered the English poet Caedmon, "sing me something." To which the poet replied, "I don't know how
to sing."[101] It was a word of weight because nobody
wanted to write it, to shoot a crow for it, to bother the
neighbours. Words demanded rocks, a tortoise shell,
a camel's hide, blood, bones, light, space, will. Yet we
write them, carry them, kill for them. Allah explains
to Muhammad: "Had We sent down this Quran upon
a mountain, you would have certainly seen it humbled

and torn apart in awe."[102] So we take the burden, and we rip it from within us before it tears us apart.

However, I think I might be wrong. I think things like words and beetles and snow, no matter how numerous, will always maintain a heaviness. I am not sure I know how to prove this, but Edward Wilson, on his exhibition to Antarctica, carried a copy of the works of Tennyson with him. After reading *In Memoriam A.H.H.*, he wrote in his diary, "if the end comes to me here or hereabout…all will be as it is meant to be."[103] Maybe we write not to unclog a sink but to make the pain of having a clogged sink more bearable. I want to know these things. Tonight, I'll try to catch my brain talking. I'll try to hear it purring and understand.

Friday:

I have placed plants in my room like a sundial. Depending on which leaf the sun through my window is illuminating, I can tell exactly what hour it is. Today, it was 8 p.m. all day long. I spend the day in my bed.

Saturday:

The moon is back from Latvia. I leave my bed and run to it. I run along the river, all the way down to the Bow Falls, until I am face to face with it. I find it rising from behind Mount Rundle, white and waiting on the writing desk. I look at the moon and learn that some beauty is so very terrifying. I look at it and I am on the moon, in the moon, over the moon. This whole scene, the serene beam uninterrupted by clouds, the distant sound of cracking ice, wind rubbing against wind, trees casting their long shadows on the snow like powerlines. Do I let the bird out? Do I dare be sincere? Everything here, from frost dust to sleeping spruces, has better odds at being literature than anything my hands can pat. The stars, the stars, and the darkness in between. It's all too quiet. Do they lose their heaviness if I waste them like this? What if I carry my typewriter while I go up the mountain, what if I knew the weight of the tablets, what if I twist the neck of a magpie? A moon river slithers on the Bow River. A friend told me once that if a moon river extends from horizon to shore, it solidifies, and one can walk on it. I jump in the November water. I can't read, can't write. Look, I can't even speak. This moon river, you have to be there to see it. It is beyond all words. No description does it justice. Language fails at its sight. Unbelievable. Unimaginable. Glorious. Heavy.

I pray for lightness.

SIGNS

I was lost in the lines of a subalpine fir's trunk when I heard rattling in a branch above me. In the fraction of a second that it took me to react and look up, nothing had remained of nature's ebullition except for the swaying of a pestered bough and an arrow of snow shot towards my eyes. What was it? A squirrel, a magpie, an oread, a tengu? I couldn't be solipsistic even if I wanted to. Things seem to only happen outside of me. A friend once asked me, "Did you see the meteor shower?" I squinted. "It's nighttime already?"

I walk out of the woods. Yesterday's snow covers the mountains like a pile of dirty linen. In the winter, the mountains become aware of their nakedness. The snow falls and contours their faults, accentuating their cracks. In the summer, trees are brushed into a meld of green, and boulders are dappled by sun and clouds. While in the winter, the snow points out every furrow, every crevice, every bruise. The snow blots and mars and flays and the mountain stands, like Eve, pulling the clouds to cover its shame, waiting for rain to be its purdah. I walk under it, smirking. A passerby wearing a jacket that both zips and buttons up asks me if I saw the avalanche. I curse my curse.

I find fresh pine marten tracks; I follow. Being so light, it is very rare for a pine marten to leave any tracks, but the snow makes them easier to spot. In the summer, a circus can trot these woods and no one would notice, but in the winter, the slyest of mice turns the ground into a war zone. Tracking, however, is not an easy art. The snow will show you when a thing disturbs it, but it will never tell you what that thing was. The snow makes tracks more visible, but it will garble the print by making it larger or smaller. It's the best game winter offers, and one accepts the game by getting down on his knees to gage. A common tracking mistake is to isolate one track from the others. Single tracks can be seen as that of a coyote, a small wolf, a large fox, or even a dog. To know the difference, one must examine the gait pattern. On rare occasions when the animal leaves some scat, the tracks become of secondary importance, and the tracker must take his nose out of the tracks and into the scat. Scat is an animal's diary. Art Pearson, a Canadian biologist, wanting to know how many soapberries a grizzly bear consumes a day, followed an adult bear and collected its scat to count the seeds in it. The answer was 200,000.[104] I have read about trackers who are able to know how far an animal has gone and where it was feeding just by looking at its droppings. Scat, unlike

meteor showers and avalanches, is not one of nature's
fleeing wonders. It will sit and wait for attention like
a child. The male pine marten's home range is around
three square miles, so it's normal for its tracks to cross
themselves. Aside from being light, the bottom of a
marten's foot is very hairy, which obscures its print
and makes it even more difficult to identify. I know
it's a marten not because of a repository of tracking
knowledge I carry in my brain, but because I've seen,
on multiple occasions, a marten scavenging the near-
by grounds of the Rimrock hotel where tourists sometimes leave food behind. The best way to know an animal is to follow it, to see what makes it turn, run, roll,
to know how far it is willing to chase a squirrel, how
desperate it is for a far-reaching berry, and how lonely
it is for a companion. To read about an animal is to no
longer know it, no longer discover it, but to track an
animal is to become it. Tracking, nonetheless, can also
be a false teacher. I have followed a fox before only to
find out it was, in fact, not a fox at all, but a Shiba Inu
trying to find its owner. I keep my eyes on the track.
I go over a rock, around a tree, and then I stop by an
overlook where the tracks loop and continue west. I
wonder if the marten stopped to have a look at the
valley under. I wonder if it cares. I care, I stop, I marvel. The woods here appear dead, but once you learn
to read its signs – to know why a twig is broken, why
a tree is debarked, why the ground is dug – the woods

suddenly become crowded with life. Life, like a laced shoe, is tangled in signs; depending on what you pull, you either knot or unravel. Saint Augustine defines a sign as "a thing which causes us to think of something beyond the impression the thing itself makes upon the senses."[105] To the saint, a sign is what it signifies. Tracks are nothing but what they indicate, a fisher, a fox, a faun. Augustine divides signs into two categories: natural and conventional. Natural signs are those that signify without intention, "like smoke which signifies fire…the track of a passing animal, and the face of one who is wrathful or sad." Conventional signs, on the other hand, are "those which living creatures show to one another for the purpose of conveying."[106] As in word or song or dance. To Augustine, when a soldier hears the trumpet, the soldier knows whether to flee or advance, and when a child sees his father nodding at him, he knows that he gained approval. One can say then that the only difference between a frog's tracks and Dante's *Divine Comedy* is intention. But intention is not intrinsic neither to the sign nor the signifier. Sumerians thought that bird tracks were messages from the gods, because their marks resembled cuneiform letters, and Muslims believe that shooting stars are spears thrown by angels. Perhaps a frog's tracks to other frogs are a poem, and perhaps the *Divine Comedy* to the frog is what the frog scat is to us: a desperate sign crying for attention.

I follow the tracks for hours until they end at a pine tree. This marten either has wings or knows how to shapeshift into a leaf. I walk back home and watch the sun setting behind Norquay Mountain. If tracks signify life, light signifies sun, then what is it that this white mountain is pointing at? What is it trying to say? Am I to flee, advance, or dance? I look away, like Moses's people, unable to bear the question, but I am distracted from the question with another. What about me? Am I the smoke or the fire, the sign or the signifier? Am I *I* or another, a twirling feather, a chewed heather, God's ichor, the snow to the winter, the circle or the centre? Am I neither, not an image nor its mirror, not the dance nor its dancer. Am I forever, or a thing that was never. A magpie, poem, scat?

SHIPS LIKE MOUNTAINS;
MOUNTAINS LIKE CLOUDS

I used to sit behind my blue mullions and think up
answers. Now the blue is frayed by frost, and I know
better than to ask. The cold shuts me up the way it
does a squirrel's eyes. The duck flew away, the deer disappeared into a different dimension, and the bear dis-
sipated hair by hair. Winter like a cricket only wants
to hear its own song, so I toss and turn in my torpor.
The heater doesn't work. I turn the oven on and keep
its door open. There are spruces outside my window,
their green augur rumours of summer. I read about
microwaves. The words keep me warm: exposure to
energy, boiling point, overheating. The books stacked
by my bed are an amalgamation of African travel bro-
chures, science journals about volcanoes, and essays
on hell. I try to avoid the mystics who believe in hell
as a symbol. I avoid the uninspiring who believe in a
hell unimaginable. To Baha'is, hell is the absence of
God, to Bernard Shaw, it is a place where people are
distracted from eternity by pleasure and luxury, and
to Sikhs, it is a state of emotional attachment and
doubt. But allegories are for the mind, and the flesh is

cold. I want the roasting, the melting, the eye-gouging heat, the hissing silver spikes and gnashing of teeth, the rivers of flames and waterfalls of sulfur. The fire, Gehenna, "where the false prophets will be,"[107] where I'll find my spruces.

When the authors of the *Mahabharata* asked, "Of all the world's wonders, which is most wonderful?" they perhaps didn't anticipate Tertullian's answer, that the greatest of all wonders is "the last and eternal judgment of the universe." To Tertullian, hell is the miracle of all miracles. He writes:

> How shall I admire, how laugh, how rejoice, how exult, when I behold so many proud monarchs, and fancied gods, groaning in the lowest abyss of darkness; so many magistrates who persecuted the name of the Lord, liquefying in fiercer fires than they ever kindled against the Christians; so many sage philosophers blushing in red hot flames with their deluded scholars; so many celebrated poets trembling…so many tragedians, more tuneful in the expression of their own sufferings; so many dancers.[108]

I turn the oven off and I dance. Thy kingdom come. The French author Georges Perec, who wrote an entire novel without using the letter *E*, said that man is the most marvelous invention: "He can blow on his hands to warm them up, and blow on his soup to cool it down."[109] But such an invention fails here. My hands are cold, and my tea is colder. Muir only ate bread and tea; he said it was enough. I have no option but to believe the bluff. The pine outside is dead, the frog is dead, the sun is dead, but the fruit fly thrives in my room. What is it eating? I want what it's having. I follow it, but it leads me nowhere. A few days ago, I woke up to a spider in the corner of my kitchen. And now there are mice in the vents. Is there food here, or a flood out there? Is this a plague, or the ark?

I go out when out allows it, and I search for things that before were within my reach: streets, trees, mountains. Grey gulped the world whole. The clouds are an eclipse of moths that flutter and crash into hills and grass and each other. They rise to die in the sun only to kill it. The *Ramayana* epic tells us that mountains used to fly like clouds, that "mountains had wings" until the god Indra cut them off out of fear that they would fall on people and kill them. The Quran tells us that among God's signs "are ships like mountains." A mountain is like a ship not because it's towering, as the Mufassirun believed, but because it sinks. Buoyancy demands it. When snow falls, it weighs on the mountain and pushes it down to the earth. The mountains have sunk, soared, but come spring, they will jump out of the earth like dandelions, they will fly back with the finches.

In the streets there are ravens as bored as the trees,

so I run at them to brighten their day, but they are too cold, too old for play. A raven can live for 20 years. That's enough winters to make anything apathetic. I once saw a raven sit in the middle of the road staring down at its talons. When a truck came, the raven didn't budge, it only moved to catch the wheels of the driver who was trying to avoid it. I read somewhere that a raven will stir an ant colony then sit on it, and as the hundreds of aggravated ants crawl and cover its body, how the raven revels, how laughs, how rejoices, how exults. No one knows why they do such a thing, but a lack of meaning might be the meaning. I go down to the river and I see them perched on some pines. We don't ask each other questions. We wait for the river to do a trick, for snow to turn into ants, but the world is too cold to move and too old to play. The raven goes back to the curb, and I go back to my window.

The oven is not enough, so I read to warm my fingers. I read about Josef Tödtling, an Austrian stuntman who holds the world record for crossing the longest distance while being pulled by a horse and having his entire body ablaze. He managed to cross 500 metres at a speed of 35 kilometres per hour. I used to sit by my window and think of answers, but now I know better than to ask why. Some write novels without vowels, others sit on colonies of angry ants. Some set their bodies on fire, and others spend the winter

here. Try the world and like a carousel it'll make your
head go round. I waste my dime on something else.

LOVE IS A BURNING MANTIS

My hands have been feeling empty, and the days are getting warmer. I've been thinking about love, and I mean the noun as a newt would. After the snow, a female newt will return to her pond, and before even stretching her neck, the males come rushing. They cling to her like fire. Dozens of feet jump at her forming a ball of hormonal mayhem. The competition is often so fierce that the female suffocates under the desperate bellies of her suitors. In the water, the newts know no compromise. In my hands, there is not a sign of writhing. Even now as I stretch them to feel the snow, I bring them back to my pockets before they can catch a thing. I have always liked my breathing uninterrupted, so I stay at the shore of this collective falling. Suffering, we are told, is the root of life, but that is only for those who participate in living. There is no loss in neutrality. To enjoy life we only need not to enjoy it too much. How can I tell you without sounding mad, that the opposite of anything is exactly the thing itself. Time, the cliché claims, is not a line but a loop, and I am beginning to believe that the same goes for the mind. Edwin Bernbaum writes that "mystics often speak of their experience of divine love as a scorching heat,"[110] but so do dwellers of hell speak of God's wrath. We are faced with a burning whether from love or its absence. It is fire no matter where we go.

Horror, too, is both the reaction to extreme ugliness and extreme beauty. In everything that intensely attracts us is something that secretly repels us. We fear what we worship as much as we fear what we detest. When the early mountaineers first encountered the Rockies, they were crippled by contradiction. They didn't understand why they felt joy in such desolation. They were never more alone, and never more alive. The feeling can perhaps be explained by realizing that the most horrifying nightmares and the most beautiful dreams both require a darkness. In everything that intensely attracts us is something that secretly terrifies us. We fear what we worship as much as we fear what we detest, and since we run from spiders and avoid climbing cliffs, it seems that sometimes our fear of things saves their lives and sometimes it saves ours, but which fear do we hold when we run from love? I don't know. Nonetheless, I have been running. Nonetheless, it is a life saved. In the world, nothing is more difficult than waking up every day to the insanity of two extremes and choosing to remain somewhere in between. If I let go and lean, I will be caught, as Robert Frost predicted, in blazing heat or scorching ice. We are assured, of course, that burning is necessary for regrowth, that love feels like a fire because it breaks us open to pull something that otherwise would not come out. In a famous prayer, Muhammad supplicated for that fire: "God, let there be fire in my heart, fire on my tongue, fire in what I see, fire in what I hear. Let there be fire on my right, fire on my left, fire above me, fire below me, fire within me, let me be fire." But God of fire, not all of us have serotinous hearts. I fear the fire as much as I do the cold, but my hands have been feeling old, and I am starting to think that it is time to risk it all, to let go of the centre, to worship the drowning deities. What is on my left is also exactly on my right, all I need to do is turn, turn like the world, like a merry-go-round, like the blood around my aorta.

In his book, *A Guide to Native Bees of Australia*, entomologist Terry Houston reports how males of the Dawson's burrowing bee wait impatiently for a female to emerge from its hole, a hole she had made a home for almost a year. When the female crawls out of the darkness – her face white and clueless – she is outnumbered a hundred to one. "Pounced on by the waiting males," Houston observes, "a buzzing ball forms which tumbles about on the ground."[111] Legs and wings and feverish eyes surround the lone female. In the frenzy of passion, she often loses a leg, an eye, a head. Consider the brown antechinus, another animal native to Australia, who, when mating season comes, runs from one female to another until its heart bursts from exhaustion. Or the nursery web spider that is eaten by the female if she rejects him and is eaten by her if she welcomes him. Or the Labord's chameleon that is killed by the female after mating, or by its own hormones if it doesn't mate, or by other males if, miraculously, it manages to survive both. What have we, with our Helens and Cleopatras, to show in the scale of love? We are often told that life without the charm of love is not possible, but I want to argue an alternative view. I want to argue that love without the risk of death is not possible either. "I don't want to live," wrote Zelda Fitzgerald to her husband, "I want to love first, and live incidentally."[112] To love is to test your lungs, to cross your fingers and throw yourself in the pond of mayhem, in the ball of frenzy. Cleanth Brooks, paraphrasing John Donne, writes that "one does not expect to live by love, one expects, and wants, to die by it."[113] Consider Julie de Lespinasse who claimed to have loved Hippolyte de Guibert "to excess, to distraction,"[114] and died of grief when he married another. Or Qays Ibn al-Mulawwah, a Bedouin who loved a girl named Layla so intensely that he was nicknamed "Al-Majnun," the idiot. When news reached him that Layla had been betrothed to another, he walked under the Sahara sun until it scorched him to death. Two verses were found etched on a rock by his body:

I pray my love never loves
To not suffer what lovers endure.

It is not the death of love that kills the lover, death is a prerequisite to love, a part of it. In Pliny the Elder's *Natural History, Volume VIII*, we are told how in the summer dragons crave the cold blood of elephants, so they travel to Africa and fall on them from the sky, coil around them like a knot, and then sink their teeth into their throats. When the dragon is filled, it lets go of the elephant who, being bled by the dragon, quickly collapses to its death, trapping the dragon under its weight and crushing it down with it. Both elephant and dragon writhe in the mud until they die; the former from injury and the latter from entanglement. Love comes to us like the teeth of a dragon. It is not the letting go that kills us, but the first touch, the moment of collision, the sinking in. To keep the dragon alive, we must teach it that holding is a thing forever, and to keep the elephant alive, we must convince it not to resist the pain. After the embrace, there can only be two as one or none at all. "I want to melt into you, to be so terribly close to you that my own self disappears," wrote Anaïs Nin to June Miller. "I am full of an acute, awesome joy. It is the joy one feels when one has accepted death and disintegration, a joy more terrible and profound than the joy of living."[115] When we merge, we kill to make room for life, we burn to turn into evergreens, we let go to be held, and anyways, if we cannot kill what horrifies us, why not just kill the part of us that cannot accept the horrible?

On the bridge by Muskrat Street, you can see mountains behind the mountains, their peaks, when the sun
is at its lowest, glow like teeth. It's February 14th. I sit
by the river and wait for something to fill my hands,
to stomp me with its feet. The snow has melted. I'm
still searching. It was the Romans who originated the
idea of Valentine. On the 14th of February of every
year, they celebrated the feast of Lupercalia where
men would sacrifice animals and run naked smearing
the blood of their sacrifices on women as they passed
them. It was believed that such a ritual would make
the women fertile. On the bridge, a female passes.
She's wearing red for love. Red for fire. Red for blood. I
fear for her lungs. The male next to her grins. I dismiss
it as a coincidence that baboons smile as a sign of ag-
gression. For millions of years it has been nature's mission to make the sexes more appealing to each other,
to make things get going. Green plumage and manes
and mustaches. The girl shades her eyelashes black to
make them look bigger. Female long-tailed dance flies
fill their abdomens with air to make them larger. The
males like that. Her mate likes that. I follow them until
the ritual. They enter the altar, the trembling taber-
nacle. Tens of people fill a room red with an air that
almost veils. Everyone's teeth are white and moving.
There is so much leather – spread on a wall, dead on
the couch, trampled by feet. There is so much flesh –
cheeks and thighs and bare shoulders. The noise has

knuckles, and it bruises. The faces shine like polished brass, and the bodies are shaking, shaking, shaking. This is a *puja*. Everyone's hands are swaying. I came for a covenant that no one promised me. The suitors wait by the door for someone to stretch their neck, but love here, unlike a newt's, has nuances. One doesn't rush, he dances. A female approaches me. Her hips wobbling like a lyrebird. I show her some teeth. She offers me her lips. Her belly against mine has no weight. My legs around hers risk nothing. Our hands are cold and hesitant. We untangle and our heads are still intact. "For God so loved the world, that he gave his one and only Son."[116] It was a principle; only the possibility of death can maintain the purity of love. I go back to the river with no scars to show, and I hear all the fish laughing.

Consider the praying mantis, an insect whose habits of love made Jean-Henri Fabre conclude in his study of mantises, "The mantis, I fear, has no heart."[117] Consider how it searches in the tall grass for a female, and when it finally finds one, it approaches coyly and slowly from behind. The female is often twice the male's size and is known for a specific appetite for male mantises' heads. Eating the male after mating increases fecundity. The male is fully aware of this sexual cannibalism. He knows the risk, the difficulty, yet his legs, despite his head, despite rumours of death, move forward, and, like Protesilaus, he leaps to his fate. Possessed by a burning, he clings to her wings and initiates his dance. The female lifts her stomach and allows him the embrace. When their bodies sway as one, the female rotates her head and begins munching her mate's head, starting with his eyes all the way to the neck. The male doesn't budge, doesn't hesitate. He only wants to love first and live incidentally. His rhythm, headless or not, remains the same. Over his gnawed shoulders, his hands twitch at the sky. This is euphoria. This is *fanaa*. Naming it the praying mantis, wrote Fabre, was a great mistake: "The pious airs are a fraud; those arms raised in prayer are really the most horrible weapons…The Mantis is fierce as a tigress, cruel as an ogress."[118] But it takes a poet, not a scientist, to know the name of things. Coleridge writes, "He prayeth best, who loveth best."[119]

I have been praying lately, and I've been thinking of you. Tea, with hibiscus, I remember by the window, and there were climbing pothos and faded frames, and stained sheets and candles. I found you between tall grass and pastels, and like biscuits in milk we melted, and anywhere we went I loved you, and you, I think, loved to lie on rocks by a creek. It has been years since then, but I hear rumours that if a chance might come, it'll come only after death, and so I've been trying to die as fast as I can. What can I say, yes, you drove me to the edges of my sanity, but you also cut my hair, sat with my silence, and touched me right.

Every night your small fingers held mine on a bed that barely held us, and every night we gave love with hearts that barely kept us. You and I were like this, refugees in love; we managed on flickers, and our love was precious because it slept dying and woke up a miracle, so we pitied it like a crippled dog, and on and on it went: me drying mint by the window, you picking lint from the floor, us lying bent on the sofa. We tried our nakedness like our youth and played peek-aboo with our hate, then laughed when it came and scared us. I washed your feet, and you bloomed in my head. You spilled coffee and blood on my bed. "So what?" you said, but sometimes in my room with the slant of winter light on our floral sheets I swear that the answer is somewhere. I had you in my heart, and you had me in your hands. It was good for a time, but when you turned your head, I feared for mine. I had to, before you had me. My Layla, what have I undone? If on a night you happen to be passing here, I pray, like a mantis, come end what you have begun.

ASK NOW THE BEAST

The promise of pogrom makes me run, grinning, tongue out, after a map of fox prints beaded in yesterday's snow like an argument. They were right, neither Emerson nor Flaubert can civilize a man. Nazis read Melville and still, well, remained Nazis. I read the Vedas for breakfast, and still I run to gloat at blood, to witness war. The fox began, leisurely, sinking his weight in shallow snow. The scattered prints of the chevron-shaped callus heels are unique to foxes. Wherever a fox trots, its heels stamp the earth with *I am a fox, I am a fox*, "*What I do is me.*"[120] The four paws repeat themselves iambically. They trail south without pause until the clean claws and careful steps morph into a jumbled salsa dance; who knows finesse in the face of hunger? The fox's tracks lace with a rodent's. They waltz up, up a hill, around some twigs, under white arched branches. The prints meet and melt into one another. There is no telling who's who. The fox no longer names itself a fox. Aristotle believed that men become animals when driven by desire, but what becomes of animals? Prey and predator swirl like dervishes gyrating a constellation. I follow the confused

creation around a berry shrub. The northern hemi-
sphere is decorated with a fox who became the Canis
Minor. If this chase continues longer, I fear Zeus's im-
patience. The tracks merge and overlap, and then, on
a white sheet of frost, blood. The rodent is no longer,
and the fox is a fox again. Over a distant spruce I spot
the culprit red and bright like a pimple. Its raised tail
is thick and long, and its short ears are turned out-
ward. It throws an uninterested look towards me and
runs again after another scent, grinning, tongue out.
I stand over the blood remembering the Vedas, "It's
impossible for fools to tread the path of learned ones."
The fool follows again.

I came out searching for prairie crocuses. The
pale-purple flowers are the toes of spring, dipped
first to test the waters. If they bloom all right, spring
cannonballs the woods. But the fox made me forget
the flowers, the frost, and myself. It ran ahead like
a memory, vivid until it's gone. In Lewis Carroll's
Through the Looking-Glass, a book I understood as a
child but found impossible as an adult, Alice wanders
into a forest "where things have no names." She walks
in and immediately forgets the names of woods and
trees and herself: "Who am I? I will remember, if I can!
I'm determined to do it!" But being determined didn't
help much, and all she could say, after a great deal of
puzzling, was "L, I know it begins with L!"[121] A fawn
happened to be walking by and asked Alice for her

name, but she couldn't remember, so she asked for his, and he said that he'll remember when they leave the forest. "They walked on together through the wood, Alice with her arms clasped lovingly round the soft neck of the Fawn, till they came out into another open field."[122] The fawn then suddenly recalled that he was a fawn, and that Alice is a human. When the realization came to him, he "darted away at full speed."[123] I took the passage to a friend and asked his 12-year-old daughter, Violet, to explain it to me. She said, "The little deer was only pretending because she was afraid to walk in the forest alone. If not, then she would have forgotten to remember that she was forgetting!"

Under the peaks of the Three Sisters, the mountain is still deciding which season to wear. Lines of muffled green shrug winter's tyranny. Loud clouds interrupt the mountains. The wind comes stuttering. The wind speaks a language, and trees are its alphabet. The leaves like tongues vibrate against the gale to shape its utterance. In this valley, wind sings spruce until it's out of breath. The Stoney People knew how to read this language. Like Morse code, they would listen to the silence and gaps pressed by things against the wind. They knew when the breeze whispered mountain ash or kinnikinnick. I don't know any Stoney People to ask, what is the wind saying against my shoulders? There is a question that passes me like a slant of light whenever a tree creaks or a shrub shrugs, and it asks,

what? But I squint away from the question until it's
out of light. What does it matter *what* the wind is saying? Whether the wind soughs with an answer to the
cosmological constant or whistles its own name does
not matter one bit. You can spend a lifetime, and some
have, looking at Klimt's *Death & Life* pondering *what*
is it all about, *what* does it mean? And maybe you can
find an answer, but maybe I can also say, *you're wrong*,
and that's it. That's a life wasted, and for what? On a
what. I have never met anyone arguing the meaning
of clouds or apples, yet we don't find it ridiculous to
do so with life. It's an important point. One does not
wish for an orange to mean anything, one just wants it
to taste good. The leaves rustle, the birds whistle, the
hills are singing "The Sound of Music," and I ask not
what it is saying, but why does it sound good? This is
not rhetorical. I want you to answer me.

Last summer I walked up Castle Mountain. Starting
the trail to Tower Lake I couldn't focus on any of the
flora or see any of the fauna. My sight was too occupied
by the orange-robed monks who were singing hymns
and blowing incense. They were scattered around the
woods like *komorebi*. Every five minutes I would spot
a monk on a rock like a rock, under a tree like a tree,
by a pond like a sky. I worried for them. There is only
one god in these woods, and its claws know no tol-
erance. Around Tower Lake the monks fenced the
shore, this years' saplings. What were they looking

for? I walked more until I arrived at Rockbound Lake, a lake squeezed by high walls of limestone and shale. A man was sitting between a boulder that the wind had split in half. I was bothered by his silence, so I bothered him. He said that Castle Mountain is sacred, that the Buddha can sometimes be seen running around its woods like wind. He said that if we sit and listen, we would hear him, see him. I climbed the east side of the mountain listening, looking for wind. I heard a scream coming from the gorge below. I used my whistle to announce myself, and another scream echoed back. It happened; God had found one of the monks. I yelled asking for their location, but no response came. I ran up for a higher view and stood on the ledge squinting at the world below. The monk was still between the wind-split rock, waiting for wind. I whistled a long, loud note, and, to my horror, the rock next to me whistled back. I stood stolid like a rock, a tree, a sapling. Here I am, I whispered to the I am, and the rock answered. Did the bush become the wind? Had the wind become a rock? Will I be split in half? And before I took my shoes off, a yellow-bellied marmot came out, stood on its hind legs, and whistled in my face. I laughed all the way to the top.

High above the ground, the edges of the sky tuck the earth into form, and the sun, three mountains wide, imbues the clouds with deep gold. My mother would tell me often, before I left home, that like the sun, everything dies in the west. She was right, but I wish she knew how colourful death here is. Behind me, a blanket is pulled over peaks tinted like old memories. Blue is the colour of forgetfulness, and I let it cover me.

As I was walking down, I heard three marmots talking. A marmot call sounds like a plea for help, like a teapot ready for brewing. Back in the day, the fur trader nicknamed the animal the "Rock Whistler." I said hello to one of them, but it ran, so I tried a different approach with the others. I listened to their squeaking and, with my best marmotian, said, "Eeeeek." The marmot jerked forward and *eeeked* back at me. I *eeeked* again and the marmot didn't disappoint. This went on for some minutes. We were talking, speaking in tongues. It mattered not what I was speaking, it only mattered that I was spoken to. The sun was now fully behind the mountains, so I said goodbye to the marmot. I, remembering my words, said it in English, but the marmot looked at me with terror, with embarrassment, and "darted away at full speed." He ran like the wind, in the wind. Did he remember, or was he feeling alone? I'll have to ask Violet.

I remember as a child how it startled me that the pigeons in Istanbul were saying the same thing as the pigeons in Damascus. I had heard rumours about languages, and I imagined that the world took its compartmentalization more seriously. The seagulls in Turkey came wobbling for bread and begged in the same pitiable call as they did back home. I was 8 years old when the world handed me my first problem, and it went like this: A hungry seagull came to the shore and mewed for bread. Man X, who happened to be Turkish, offered it a piece of bread. The next day the seagull returned with the same intention, and Man Y, who happened to be Italian, also offered it a piece of bread. If both X and Y understand S, explain why X and Y do not understand one another. Unfortunately, I couldn't flip to the back of the book for an answer. I was driving on Vancouver Island last winter when I found it. I stopped and rolled down the window. The waves like crabs climbed one another and scurried towards the shore, and somewhere behind their noise was a noise I have heard before. I had heard it in Lahore over scarlet-splotched *salwars* on laundry lines. I had heard it in Amman, in Virginia. Only then did I think of an answer, but I muffled it like a hiccup. I was worried. What if someone simply replied, *you're wrong.* That's it. That's my life wasted. Outside the car window a girl in a yellow jacket was screaming with her hands stretched around a sequoia, "biiiiig tree." I remember yelling as a child when seeing an oak, "*shajara kabeeeeera!*" I am aware of the curse, but the builders of Babel might have outwitted their fate, because when the girl yawned, I yawned the same, and when the breeze came, she left, I drove out, and the bald eagle flew away. What's in a name? Only everything.

In a paper titled "The Silent Scream of the Lima Bean," Wilhelm Boland and Massimo E. Maffei promise that if we could hear trees, their "screams of battle would destroy any summer idyll."[124] When an insect bites a leaf or nibbles on a twig, the tree will analyze the saliva of the intruder and search for a match in the archive of insects stored in its memory. Once the attacker is identified, the tree will respond accordingly. If a caterpillar munches on the leaves of a tree, the tree will exhale a fragrance that calls out for parasitoid wasps who rush to the rescue by laying their eggs inside the caterpillars. If it's a deer who's doing the munching, the tree defends itself by shooting chemicals in the leaves that make them taste bad. Scientists also tell us that trees communicate with one another through fungal networks that stretch under the forest floor. They call it the "wood wide web." Through this web, trees will exchange nutrients, information, and even donations from richer relatives. Trees talk, as author Michael Pollan puts it, through a chemical vocabulary. This is no small discovery. Trees are talking! Trees are talking to one another, to other species, to themselves! Yeats noted, "We make out of the quarrel with others, rhetoric, but of the quarrel with ourselves, poetry."[125] I wonder if that's how a fruit is made. Are flowers soliloquies unheard? I go to gatherings and ask people, "Do you know that when a leaf speaks, its words travel through its veins at a speed of one centimetre per minute?" They think I'm passing time with chatter. I want them to scream! Can't they see, nothing is what it seems. Elephants, the giants louder than thunder, speak to one another quieter than rain. They talk through the earth by tapping it. Like the fox, their walk is a talk. An elephant miles away can pick up the seismic waves of its herd and communicate with them by using special receptors in their feet called Pacinian corpuscles, which allow them to translate vibrations. What is astonishing about this proboscidean Morse code is that both the talking and the listening are done with the same body part, the foot! What is Pegasus? Uraeus? Here, you have a beast that has in its hand a nose and its foot an ear. Trees must be relieved, for if they fall, an elephant will always hear.

If we examine communication in the animal world even further, we will find that our understanding of language and signs is as reliable as a sugar-free doughnut. Mantis shrimps use their entire body to converse through light, white rhinos use boards made of dung to leave messages, Caribbean reef squid use their skins to talk with colour, and some species of bees draw maps by wiggling. A bee, after scavenging for nectar, will return to its home and perform a choreographed dance to say things like, "head north to the woodpecker's nest and then turn left to take exit four through the twayblade tunnel following the leaf miner tracks for three minutes to arrive at your destination." Grouper fish, after losing their prey in a coral crevice, will go wake a moray eel and point them to where the prey is hiding. The eel will follow the grouper and squeeze itself in the crevice to scare the prey out of its hiding spot. The grouper will then seize the opportunity and eat the frantic fish, but, of course, only if the eel loses its chance to eat it first. While in outer space, a magazine reports that Mars is humming. What is this? Why is no one despairing? Groupers make plans with eels, trees scream at caterpillars, Mars hums to the sun, elephants talk to the earth, bees dance to one another, and we're still unsure how to pronounce *pecan*. I will go to the monk. I will tell him to get up and run. Get up and run. It's all a sham. It's upside down. You can't hear a thing until you learn how to listen with your feet. Talk with your hands? Woody Allen said, "God is silent. Now if we can only get man to shut up."[126] Nothing is silent; we've just been left out of a conversation that began millions of years ago. If anything, we're too quiet. God used to come down the mountain like a professional wrestler, with "the thunderings, and the lightning, and the noise of the trumpet, and the mountain smoking,"[127] and we heard it, but we couldn't bear it. We said, "Let not God speak with us, lest we die."[128] God didn't go mute; he muted us. It's a loud world out there, too loud to bear, too loud to hear, and we're too proud to forget our names. This is not a cappella. There is a drumming, strumming. There is an orchestra. I'm going to the mountains to chew some trees, to yell at frogs. I want to participate. I want in. Who am I? I will forget, if I can.

CHAPTER IV

SPRING

Cosmos in bloom
As if no war
Were taking place

—SUIKO MATSUSHITA

MERCY

First rain fell five days ago. The months will now have
names. It is April. Like the Pawukon calendar of the
Balinese, time here is measured locally. People don't
talk of years but of winters, and winter like Yahweh
is named through metonymy: the Season. The Season
is over after six Gregorian months, and no one seems
to question it. How can a six-month work disappear
in a day? I never seem able to witness the turning, to
wait on a season like a train. It happens so quickly; one
day you're cold, the next you're fighting butterflies off
your face. Snow melts and unmuzzles the grass. I don't
have to witness the world from behind glass anymore.
Snow melts and chaos sprouts. The animals are going insane. Everything wants to bash its head against
everything: squirrels against trees, bees against windows, elk against elk, buds against earth, rain against
the world. This din is so sudden. Who placed spring
after winter? I can easily learn to love this noise, but I
delay the love. I close the curtains. First, I must stretch
my body out of its winter. Through my window I've
seen the ears of a coyote trudging through snow. That
was it. That was my winter. But now the eyes of Argus

are too few to keep up. I must have seen twelve elk in an hour. Spring brings a surplus of life, and everyone wants it. Krill and whales and saxifrage and sequoias are all desperate for sun and air and each other. It is a life I want to want, but if I allow this abrupt heat in after a long frost, I'll shatter into myself like a mirror.

Behind the curtains green is back. Green is the colour trees hate most. They chew it and spit it back at us, and we marvel at their spew. Of all living things, trees must be strangest. John Muir saw them as prophets, Herman Hesse as preachers, and Kahlil Gibran as "poems that the earth writes upon the sky."[129] But when trees stand alone, they are neither poetic nor prophetic; they are mainly eating. From the first seconds of their life, buds open their pores and mewl for food, suckling the udders of the sun for sugar. Unweaned, they grow gluttonous and spend their days still, literally, not to waste a bite. If trees went on ad infinitum, they would have no problem drinking the sky whole.

A tree will spend most of the year fattening its leaves. It protects them from mites and bites and droughts; it bumps them with poison and water and sugar; it clings to them come rain or shine; but come winter, it tosses them like a mistake. Some trees, such as alder and ash, shed their leaves while still green, in sight of the sun. The squander floods the forest floor. Mother Nature wastes like a child. Lisa, with her small toes dangling from a hammock, turns to tell me, "I'm

wasted by the waste. Don't write that." We run to bash
our heads against some stream.

After winter, life flaunts its fervour. Five days ago,
the world wore its mornings white. Now, there are
hues that Adam was too bleary to name. Google en-
gineers, while designing web pages, tested 41 shades of
blue on a toolbar to see which shade received the most
clicks, the most attention. I wonder if this brook followed the same method. Hundreds of mosquito larvae
hook themselves on the surface and dangle like question marks. Backswimmers and water boatman are
investigating the hairs on my legs. Some water striders are here too. I read somewhere that water striders
talk to one another by making ripples, by pressing the
water like a typewriter. A friend told me that in Texas
they call them Jesus bugs. Lisa tells me that in Canada
they call them pond-skaters. I want to read what they
are preaching, but the pond is too blue to read ripples,
too blue to notice the sham. Nature is a swindler, a con
artist. It reveals its beauty in grandeur, in plain sight –
mountains and forests and sunrises and rivers. But
underneath the shining and vivid, it hides its ugliness
by shrinking it to nothingness – larvae and naiads
and fleas and cockroaches. Perhaps nothing altered
the image the Romantics held of nature more than
the microscope. Emerson writes, "Nature never wears
a mean appearance."[130] I wonder if he had ever seen
a *Perisceptis carnivora* moth, a type of bagworm that

wears the carcasses of other bugs like a suit. I wonder if he had looked beyond the blue, beyond the trinkets of spring. Although the ear hears what it wants, the eye, unfortunately, cannot do the same. Two days ago, we had a cougar warning, and people still went out at night to walk their dogs. At home, I found a centipede in the main floor's bathroom. I used the basement's bathroom for a week. What are bears and wolves and sharks and snakes in comparison to the dragonfly larvae, the Epomis beetle, or the giant water bug that spends hours slurping the insides of frogs and fish while they are still alive. If nature had placed everything in plain sight, if we had whale-like silkworms, eagle-like wasps, wolf-like mantises, who would ever leave their curtains open?

The larches bloom in the April air. The lower part of their trunks is stripped by elk. Peter Wohlleben, the German arborist, reports that elk and deer choose the most uncommon trees in an area to rub their antlers against. Sometimes the rubbing is so intense that the trees usually don't survive it. Larches turn a perfect yellow every October, a yellow so yellow that the branches look like they are burning. Yet running comes the elk, regardless of pines and beauty, to bash its head against one of the rarest trees in the valley. Human, all too human. Orcas, after successfully hunting another whale's calf, will feast on its tongue – and only its tongue – then toss the giant mass of meat and bones aside like a bitter broccoli, while other orcas will hunt a shark and eat only its liver, a risky hunt for such a small delicacy. On the other hand, the African clawed frog will eat anything that stands in its way, including other frogs, which made them responsible for the extinction of over 100 species. Lisa eats vending-machine sushi and talks over some Jesus bugs by poking ripples in the water. She's reading a book about invertebrates. "Did you know that parrot fish eat coral and rock alike while looking for algae? You should write that."

At noon we make tea and sit in the stairway by a pupa. For two weeks we watched it wrinkle and age. Today, the case seems ready to let light in and life out. The pupa cracks as a tentative moth emerges. We witness its first breath, its birthplace, its baptism by the noise. The furrowed wings slowly unfurl, demarcating their edges. The moth, strong and large, hurls itself into its nascent life then crashes against the window and plummets to the ground. That sound, the noise of small bones cracking against glass, of a certainty unfathomably failing, must be familiar to Lisa. She shrieks. Dazed and confused, the moth takes flight and heads towards the framed sky only to be knocked down again. It flips and twirls questioning the freedom of its reflection on the glass. It rises higher than before as if announcing its kamikaze and dives down determined, but it crashes again against the clear unforeseen. It struggles and winces on the cold unfamiliar tiles before it stands for yet another attempt, but as it jumps for its new life, Lisa crushes it under the sole of her sandals. She stamps on it again and again until its wings stop spasming and the sky no longer matters. "It is the merciful thing to do," Lisa explains, "to put it out if its misery."

Lisa told me once that her cousin killed his dog out of mercy. Her cousin was Buddhist, and his dog was a good dog, so he drowned it in the bathtub. "It won't have to suffer as a dog anymore," he said, "it'll come back human." And he'll come back a god, or, perhaps, a dog? Who knows. Storks, after hatching their chicks, will pick one of them up and throw it off the nest like a plum's pit. If they don't do that, the chicks will compete for food and kill one another. One dead bird on the ground is better than two dead in the bush. It's the things we do for mercy that makes us need mercy the most. Here in the National Park, feeding a chickadee can land you a $25,000 fine, but a few miles down the road out of the Park's borders, and it's considered a nice thing to do. I read in a newspaper that a black bear walked into a home in Colorado last month and took a look inside the fridge. It then pushed its way out of the wall "like the Kool-Aid Man."[131] I wonder why don't all animals come and take a look in our fridges? Why hunt and starve when they can come to the city and familiarize themselves with us. We could feed both pigeons and vultures at the park, pet cats and bears behind dumpsters, take dogs and lynxes for a night walk.

Humans are not unique to domestication. Forest ants farm aphids in order to feed on their sugary excrete by stroking them, as if cow-milking, with their antennas to speed up the process. The ants protect their farms from predators ten times their sizes. They surround the aphids like a fence, fending them from beetles and wasps and mantises, but spit a piece of candy on the forest floor, and the ants will abandon their farms and fall at the free sugar like rain drops. Comfort is craved by both the wild and tamed. Weasels will enjoy a store-bought egg roll as much as you do, and coyotes will not refuse jerky bacon for the sake of a romanticized lifestyle. In Spain, mountains of garbage filled with organic waste surround the major cities, and the storks migrating from northern Europe to Africa find these piles of trash to be an unmatched all-you-can-eat buffet. The storks enjoy the free feast so much that they stop their journey to Africa and spend the winter filling themselves up on fast food. Some storks get so comfortable that they no longer return to their homeland but continue living the rest of their happy lives in Spain. Zoologist Lucy Cooke notes that even the Eurasian blackcap, the traditional migrating bird of Britain, stopped migrating altogether due to a "steady supply of food from bird feeders."[132]

At every turn nature seems to be refusing its wilderness. And why wouldn't it? We certainly have.
Yuri Tolochko, a Kazakhstani bodybuilder, married
his pink-haired silicon sex doll. When he goes to the
beach, she follows. When he's at the gym, she's there.
When he's in the mood for some lovin', she's in the
mood too. "She doesn't fuss." An entomologist on the
radio reported how male butterflies will overlook a
female butterfly in favour of a bigger, more colourful mate made of cardboard. The male butterfly will
fly past the anticipating female and stick to the cardboard without shame. She doesn't fuss. A magpie on
the spruce outside wakes us up every day to call its
mate. Lisa is making a papier-mâché magpie with the
colours of a peacock. We're hoping for the best.

The law in the park demands that a bear must be
shot if it comes in contact with human food. "A bad
bear" is the label for a soon-to-be-dead bear. A bad
bear as opposed, I suppose, to a good bear. Most bears,
however, originally came to this area due to food
spills caused by the Canadian Pacific Railway trains,
and each year multiple bears die from crashing into
them, earning the trains the nickname "the meat min-
cers," but whether minced bears are good bears or
bad bears, it is difficult to say. Medieval Europeans,
like park administrators, thought of nature in moral
terms. Elephants, for example, were commended for
their virtue and wisdom. They were even believed to

have their own religion. Vultures, on the other hand, were condemned by the Old Testament as "an abomination among the birds."[133] The bat was equated with the devil, cats with demons, and doves with angels. Lady Jacaume of Bayonne, in 1332 France, was burnt alive for having crowds of bats living near her home. Humans may have harnessed the energy of the sun, walked on the surface of the moon, split the atom, and mapped the sky, but when it comes to understanding nature, we are no more than children reading hieroglyphics and mistaking them for a beef stew recipe. So we walk around, stumbling over one another, bashing our heads against each other; bears breaking walls and moths breaking against windows and frogs eating frogs and humans drowning dogs as God shakes his head, delaying his mercy on us.

CIRCLES

There are things small enough that light forgets not to pass, but not small enough for life. Things like algae and dinoflagellates and rotifers. Things that when looked at are looked through. Things that take the shape of the world. In the Bow River, the water is flooded by such populations. Lives that we only recently knew to be possible. Lives that give emptiness another meaning. By the moon nothing is visible, and I wonder if we will ever begin to consider that there might be things large enough that our vision forgets not to pass. I am just starting to learn, or relearn, the meaning of forms; how some shapes are easier to taste than others, how branches and words mean the same thing, and how the darkness around the moon is also the moon. I am also beginning to learn the meaning of formlessness; how the fire-hollowed oak is the ghost of smoke, how home is a space between two shoulders, and how the weight of anything is much heavier as an absence. Land is a child you grow with who remains young while you shed your skin. I have given this valley five years of my life. That is enough time for a tree to know that it is not going anywhere. My ears are not what they used to be, and the Ethiopian man who used to smoke by my window is now gone, but the spruces where he sat still smell the same. I am told that glaciers spend their days barely moving dust, but they spend their lives moving mountains. Recently, glaciers have been moving into themselves a few inches a year, moving themselves into nothing. Recently, we discovered that the whole wide earth is like a birch colony. If one tree falls, they all. Recently, I have been told that everything is dying, but wasn't it always? The chokecherries by the church died four times in four years, and I, too, like the glacier, have been going into myself a day a year, and soon I know I'll disappear. But unlike the glacier, no one is losing their breath over mine. I might not have been born to move mountains, but everyday I was moved by them. In a few days I'll stir some dust until I am standing in it, and I'll move in a sea of plankton, in herds of breathing animals that were never possible, and the light will pass me the same. Who knew emptiness had a heart that beats? Now I have become a volvox; now I have become the world. Ask me what I have spent my life on, and I'll point to the glacier, whatever it says, that is what I say.

Is it normal that I often find myself living the present as a memory? I look at newly forming clouds as if I am remembering them. Life does not unfold, does not unfurl like a lily. It loops around like a magpie who, despite the seeming ceaseless space, does not go beyond the riverbanks. The days don't either. When they arrive at the shore, they turn around and pretend to marvel at what they know. But after love there is no love, only comparison. Spring now comes like a homemade cherry pie. "One time it was warmer." "One time it smelled better." "One time it was drier." I have been walking all my life only to find out that, like a carousel horse, I was not walking at all but only going up and down in circles.

***

Yesterday I had a dream that Noah was building a flood. Despite the lack of arks, I woke up like a sea star, unmoved, on my back, looking up. For years a sea star lies without moving. Then one day, one of its arms breaks off and walks away, and the sea star doesn't notice. It sits still on the same bed. Last night it rained from dusk to Calgary. Today I woke up to a forest drowning. Spring had overworked the river. So much can happen in a night. Gil Pérez slept in Manila and woke up in Mexico. Joseph slept in a well and woke up in Egypt. My mother tells me that her father slept in Damascus and woke up in Eden. I've been sleeping on the same bed for some years now. I keep an eye on my arm.

I go down to the woods to read, but the river is sitting in my chair. The storm combed the earth and uprooted the trees that refused to part. There's mud everywhere. Spring passed here without wiping its feet. A squirrel sits stunned on a park bench. It slept yesterday on a branch that the river is now pulling across Canmore. The birds fly above and then dissolve like sugar. I only see their shadows thrown from tree to tree. I see darkness, then a flapping flicker, then nothing at all. The river is on it too. It pushes something out then pulls it back under its sleeve. There is no drumroll, no juggling to set the mood, just a pizzazz-less *pop* and then a *poof* – thank you for coming.

I spot a mourning cloak butterfly untangling itself from a web of sunrays. Its gilt-hemmed wings are strips of velvet and dots of cyan. With every flap it draws attention to itself like a poem. This is beauty – *flap* – this is beauty. I run after it to watch it, but when I run, it runs too. Unlike other aerials, butterflies don't glide, they dither, and my eyes, attempting to follow, jitter, but the careening colours, yielding to one another, dazzle, and I wonder, what it would feel like to have my edges made of gold, to wake up makeup ready, with dotted arms, a painted face, and a body tinged with a page from a Pantone. In nature, however, the function of a colour is not to please but to talk. If you stroll the woods without judging things by their cover, you will most certainly poison yourself. Butterflies often dot their wings with blue or stripe them with orange to tell a hovering bird that they are poisonous, or, at least, not worth the bite. The mourning cloak continues fluttering until it disappears into thin rays, and the woods begin to play its favourite game on me: look here, look there, it's a butterfly, a falling leaf, a deer, or maybe a drop of dew. And I run, like a child, believing the trick, and whenever I know that this time I have guessed correctly, a hand opens, and there is nothing in it at all. I don't want forever; I only want a now for two seconds.

In the woods, like in a sumo ring, you must take your shoes off and wrestle, wrestle, wrestle until a bush twists the hollow of your thigh and daybreak blesses you. A Clark's nutcracker swoops over me and sings. It flies as if it never knew a corner. Another butterfly glitches into the scene. It moves slowly, it moves wholly. This is now, and it is what everyone ever wants; not to be in the moment, but to be the moment. Not to think that you feel, but to feel that you feel. The words *mystery* and *mystic* come to us from the Greek *muein*, which means to shut one's eyes, to shut one's mouth. I shut my memories and I forget that life was anything but now. In the beginning was a word that I never knew how to read, but the word is with a butterfly that flutters by my mouth, and I sing it sweet, slowly, holy. Jack London writes, "There is an ecstasy that marks the summit of life, and beyond which life cannot rise. And such is the paradox of living, this ecstasy comes when one is most alive, and it comes as a complete forgetfulness that one is living."[134] I am now, and

if in an hour I am still now, then I have passed this
evanescence.

There are fewer birds in the park now. Every day a
sparrow wakes up to find that his home had turned
into a hotel. Paradoxically, the hotel is built to host
people who come to see the sparrow's home. A taxi
driver in Montreal told me a riddle once: What feels
smaller the bigger it gets? I forgot the answer, but I
know that the firmaments are expanding, yet the sparrow seems serried. In the late 1800s, the sky of the
New World was crowded with the passenger pigeon,
a species so successful that they accounted for nearly 40 per cent of the entire bird population of North
America. John James Audubon, the famous American
ornithologist, was travelling in a wagon when a flock
of passenger pigeons passed him, but to call it a flock
is to do it injustice. Audubon writes:

> The air was literally filled with Pigeons; the light
> of noon-day was obscured as by an eclipse, the
> dung fell in spots, not unlike melting flakes of
> snow; and the continued buzz of wings had a
> tendency to lull my senses to repose…I cannot
> describe to you the extreme beauty of their aer-
> ial evolutions, when a Hawk chanced to press
> upon the rear of a flock. At once, like a torrent,
> and with a noise like thunder, they rushed into a
> compact mass, pressing upon each other towards
> the centre. In these almost solid masses, they

darted forward in undulating and angular lines, descended and swept close over the earth with inconceivable velocity, mounted perpendicularly so as to resemble a vast column, and, when high, were seen wheeling and twisting within their continued lines, which then resembled the coils of a gigantic serpent…As soon as the Pigeons discover a sufficiency of food to entice them to alight, they fly around in circles, reviewing the country below. During their evolutions, on such occasions, the dense mass which they form exhibits a beautiful appearance, as it changes its direction, now displaying a glistening sheet of azure, when the backs of the birds come simultaneously into view, and anon, suddenly presenting a mass of rich deep purple.[135]

It was estimated that between three to five billion passenger pigeons occupied the sky of America, which at the time was double the world human population. After 50 years of the arrival of Europeans, not a single pigeon remained. In his book, *The Encyclopedia of Vanished Species*, David Day crowns the passenger pigeon with "the most astonishing and unbelievable of all extinctions."[136] Five billion dead in 50 years. My father used to claim that when he was my age, he saw more of the world in a day than I see in a month. I wonder how much more will I see than my children?

I see a squirrel with something in its hand. I see a

bee by a brook with powder on its wings. I run after
them, but it's not enough to quench the wonder. In
the winter, I had tea, and it was enough. In the spring,
I want to haul some hills across the earth. If I had to
choose between a life of calm and the chaos of spring
that drives me mad, every day I'll choose the spring.
There is wind, there is a tree, there is a mountain, and
there is me. And the wind breaks the tree, and the tree
breaks the mountain, and the mountain breaks the
wind. Is this all by an auteur, or do I participate? In the
sky and in a tennis court, above and east, on the pine-
cone and on the pebble. It's happening everywhere.
This is a ceremony, and everything is in communion.
The clouds are working with the aphid, and the ocean
conspires with the krill. There is inspiration in the
way a bough bends just right when a squirrel heaves
itself on it. There is immolation in the supple purple
of dawn against the palpitating pink of morning. This
is what St. Matthew knew; that before Adam came,
the lily was here, and after Christ passed, the lily still
grows. But Matthew, like the lily, was boiled and be-
headed. I regret that nature is a prophet as it seems
to be our nature to crucify our prophets. When Allah
wanted to create Adam, the angels asked him the same
question we've been asking: Why? The angels said,
"Will Thou place on the earth one who will corrupt it
and shed blood?"[137] I think about the angel's question

every day. Did they find an answer, or are they still scratching their halos?

The great auk is another bird who disappeared from our world forever. Although its extinction was not as astonishing as that of the passenger pigeon, it was undoubtedly more horrifying. The auk was a gentle flightless bird who resembled the penguin, except it was larger in size and had white patches over its eyes. Day writes that the bird's encounter with the Europeans was like "someone's nightmare of hell." The death of the auk is a holocaust unremembered. Thousands of them were packed into small pens next to "blistering flames that licked up into the air."[138] The assault was then carried on by five groups. The first group pushed their way through the flock while swinging spiked clubs at their squeezed skulls, the second group followed the strikers and tossed the birds over the pen's walls, the third group took the birds, some still breathing, and either threw them in a fire pit or in boiling cauldrons. "There was no wood with which to feed the flames in this place," Day writes, "so the thick insulating layer of fat which protected the birds from arctic waters served as fuel."[139] The fourth group used rakes to collect the feathers off of the boiling flesh, and the last group stabbed the naked birds with hooked poles and hurled them into the shore where thousands of rotting bodies waited for the tide to wash them away. Miraculously, the species survived the holocaust

and continued to survive the rigorous hunting of
Europeans for almost 300 years. Until the 3rd of June,
1844, when three Icelandic fishermen found the last
two living great auks who were a breeding pair with
a single egg, the last great auk egg. An egg that survived for hundreds of years despite foxes and frost and
famine. The fishermen killed the adults with clubs and
smashed the egg with their boots. Nature was too gentle a teacher to prepare the great auks for us.

Since the 1500s, over 140 species of birds have gone
extinct, 80 mammals, 10 per cent of all insects, and
around 600 plants. There seems to be not enough
world for what we want from the world. These horrifying statistics are not, as many believe, an acci-
dental consequence of industrialization or pollution.
They are as purposeful and methodical as tides. The
northern curlew was wiped out by using glass guns
developed in Nebraska, "one single shot was recorded to have dropped 28 Curlews."[140] Wolf populations
were devastated in North America by simply killing
buffalos and poisoning their carcasses with strych-
nine sulphate. The unsuspecting wolf would come
to feast on the buffalo only to drop dead on the spot.
This technique did not only kill the wolves, but anything that ate meat, "coyotes, foxes, weasels, cougars,
bears, skunks, badgers, ferrets, ground squirrels, ra-
coons, eagles, bobcats, ravens, and – not infrequent-
ly – Indians."[141] Some books make mention of wolves

that were "publicly hanged," "burnt alive," or "smashed to smithereens under rocks."[142] Today, around 1 per cent of the original wolf population remains alive in the Americas. Today, on the trail from my home to Sulphur Mountain, out of that 1 per cent, I saw a wolf running through the thick woods, and asters bloom-ing despite all the trampling. James tells us that "the testing of your faith produces steadfastness,"[143] but perhaps it is not us who are being tested but this stead-fast world.

Over the mountains, the sky kept its grey all day. The forecast is predicting rain. And now, as before, a flood is coming, and "all the fountains of the great deep burst forth."[144] We are the flood. We fall covering the mountains until "all flesh die[s] that moves on the earth, birds, livestock, beasts, all swarming creatures that swarm on the earth."[145] We fall as the angels ask why. Yet the aster, strong against its testing, is still here, and it flutters, it quivers. And the stretching sky traps, it showers. Shakespeare asks, "How with this rage shall beauty hold a plea / Whose action is no stronger than a flower?"[146] I am not certain of an answer, but I know that even if, with time, we were to lose colour and dis-integrate until our edges turn into a circle, and the cir-cle into nothingness, that everything carries within it the desire to become what made it. The direction of an apple, if given enough time, is to become a tree. What would we, after all this circling, be?

NOTES

SENESCENCE

1   Also known as Tunnel Mountain. The Stoney
    Nakoda call it Eyarhey Tatanga Woweyahgey
    Wakân, or Sleeping Buffalo, because it looks like a
    sleeping buffalo when viewed from the north.

2   Micah 1:4.

3   Natalie Rice, "Scorch," Terrain.org. https://www.
    terrain.org/2023/poetry/natalie-rice/.

4   "Georgia Politician Stands by Giant Topiary
    Chicken That Got Him Ousted as Mayor," *As It
    Happens*, CBC Radio, November 24, 2021, https://
    www.cbc.ca/radio/asithappens/as-it-happens-the-
    wednesday-edition-1.6261125/georgia-politician-
    stands-by-giant-topiary-chicken-that-got-him-
    ousted-as-mayor-1.6261128.

5   Malachi 4:1.

6   Matthew 24:7.

7   *Aṅguttara Nikāya* 7.66.

8   Mike Hulme, *Climate Change* (London: Routledge,
    2021), 239.

9   Quran 85:12–14.

.10 Daniel 8:14.

11 Daniel 9:24.

12 Revelation 13:1–18.

13 Revelation 6:12–13.

14 Roy Scranton, *Learning to Die in the Anthropocene: Reflections on the End of a Civilization* (San Franciso: City Lights Publishers, 2015), 240.

15 Sylvia Plath, *Ariel* (London: Faber & Faber, 2010), 10.

16 Abbas Amanat and Magnus T. Bernhardsson, eds., *Imagining the End: Visions of Apocalypse from the Ancient Middle East to Modern America* (London: I.B. Tauris, 2002), 26.

17 Francis Bacon, *Bacon's Essays and Wisdom of the Ancients* (Boston: Little Brown & Co., 1884), 292, https://archive.org/details/baconsessayswisdoobaco/page/n5/mode/2up.

18 Frederick W. Turner, "Cultivating the American Garden," in *The Ecocriticism Reader: Landmarks in Literary Ecology*, eds. Cheryll Glotfelty and Harold Fromm (Athens: University of Georgia Press, 1996), 43.

19 Peter Brannen, *The Ends of the World: Volcanic Apocalypses, Lethal Oceans, and Our Quest to Understand Earth's Past Mass Extinctions* (New York: Ecco, 2017), 17.

20 2 Corinthians 5:17.

21 Revelation 20:8.

22 Jeremiah 51:25.

23 Parisa Hashempour, "Why Yachting Families Make Great Climate Caretakers," *Superyacht Life*, November 3, 2021, https://thesuperyachtlife.com/purpose/

why-yachting-families-make-great-climate-care-
takers/.

24 Ian Ritchie, "How the Year without Summer Gave
Us Dark Masterpieces," *The Guardian*, June 16,
2016, https://www.theguardian.com/music/2016/
jun/16/1816-year-without-summer-dark-master-
pieces-beethoven-schubert-shelley.

25 Douglas Cole and Bradley Lockner, eds., *To the
Charlottes: George Dawson's 1878 Survey of the
Queen Charlotte Islands* (Vancouver: UBC Press,
1993), 69.

26 Cathy Caruth, *Unclaimed Experience: Trauma,
Narrative, and History*, 20th Anniversary ed.
(Baltimore, MD: Johns Hopkins University
Press, 2016).

27 Job 38:4.

GHOSTS

28 Ashley Strickland, "New Image of Colliding
Galaxies Previews the Fate of the Milky Way,"
Space's Next Chapter, CNN, August 10, 2022, https://
www.cnn.com/2022/08/10/world/colliding-gal-
axies-gemini-north-image-scn/index.html.

29 Turner, "Cultivating the American Garden," 45.

30 Lucy Cooke, *The Truth about Animals: Stoned
Sloths, Lovelorn Hippos, and Other Tales from
the Wild Side of Wildlife* (New York: Basic
Books, 2019).

THE BODY

31 George B. Schaller, "Reflections in a Hidden Land,"
in *Extreme Landscape: The Lure of Mountain*

Spaces, ed. Bernadette McDonald (Washington, DC: National Geographic, 2002), 52.

32 Mary H. Kingsley, *Travels in West Africa* (London: Macmillan & Co., 1897), 178.

33 John Muir, "Exploration in the Great Tuolumne Canon," *Sierra Club Bulletin* (Sierra Club, 1924), 73.

34 Jean-Jacques Rousseau quoted in Edwin Bernbaum, *Sacred Mountains of the World*, 2nd ed. (Cambridge: Cambridge University Press, 2022), 143.

35 Martin Buber, *I and Thou* (New York: Free Press, 1971), 16.

36 Buber, 7.

37 Iris Murdoch quoted in Natasha Lunn, *Conversations on Love: With Philippa Perry, Dolly Alderton, Roxane Gay, Stephen Grosz, Esther Perel, and Many More* (London: Viking, 2022), 229.

38 Carl G. Jung, *Memories, Dreams, Reflections*, ed. Aniela Jaffé, trans. Clara Winston and Richard Winston, rev. ed. (New York: Vintage, 1989), 20.

39 Job 5:23.

40 Christopher Manes, "Nature and Silence," *Environmental Ethics* 14, no. 4 (1992): 346–47, https://doi.org/10.5840/enviroethics19921445.

41 Gretel Ehrlich, "We Called It the Attic," in McDonald, *Extreme Landscape,* 2.

42 Schaller, "Reflections in a Hidden Land," 54.

43 Ralph Waldo Emerson, *The Essential Writings of Ralph Waldo Emerson*, ed. Brooks Atkinson (New York: Modern Library, 2000), 23.

44 Ovid, *Metamorphoses*, trans. Rolfe Humphries (Bloomington: Indiana University Press, 1960), 102.

45 Brian Patton, *Tales from the Canadian Rockies* (Toronto: McClelland & Stewart, 1993), 1.

46 Mark Forsyth, *The Etymologicon: A Circular Stroll through the Hidden Connections of the English Language* (London: Icon Books, 2011), 28.

47 Alberto Manguel, *A History of Reading* (Toronto: Vintage Canada, 1998), 21.

48 Ezequiel Martínez Estrada quoted in Manguel, *A History of Reading*, 19.

49 Jeremiah 15:16.

50 Benjamin Alire Sáenz, *Dark and Perfect Angels: A Collection of Poems* (El Paso, TX: Cinco Puntos Press, 1996), 96.

51 Luke 22:19.

52 Jeannette C. Armstrong, "Sharing One Skin: Okanagan Community," *Columbiana* 7, no. 1 (Okanogan, WA: Columbia River Bioregional Education Project, 2001), https://webcat.library. ubc.ca/vwebv/holdingsInfo?bibId=10078741.

53 Nyle C. Brady and Raymond R. Weil, *Elements of the Nature and Properties of Soils*, 3rd ed. (Upper Saddle River, NJ: Pearson, 2009), 53.

54 Brady and Weil, 53.

55 Francis Bacon, *Bacon's Essays and Wisdom of the Ancients* (Boston: Little Brown & Co., 1884), 267, https://archive.org/details/ baconsessayswisdoobaco/page/n15/mode/2up.

56 Henry David Thoreau, *The Portable Thoreau*, ed.

Jeffrey S. Cramer (New York: Penguin Classics, 2012), 344.

57 Jorge Luis Borges, *Selected Non-Fictions*, ed. Eliot Weinberger, trans. Esther Allen and Suzanne Jill Levine (New York: Penguin Books, 1999), 31.

FATHER TO THE MAN

58 Leo Tolstoy quoted in Viktor Shklovsky, *Viktor Shklovsky: A Reader*, ed. Alexandra Berlina (New York: Bloomsbury Academic, 2016), 17.

59 Shklovsky, 17.

60 Shklovsky, 18.

61 Translated from a memory of a sermon I heard once.

62 William Wordsworth, "My Heart Leaps Up," poets.org, https://poets.org/poem/my-heart-leaps.

63 Mansur al-Hallaj, "I Am the Truth" *(Anal-Haq) Diwan of Mansur al-Hallaj*, trans. Paul Smith (CreateSpace Independent Publishing Platform, 2016).

64 Corinthians 12:9–10.

HEAVINESS

65 Exodus 10:5.

66 Anne Fadiman, *Ex Libris: Confessions of a Common Reader* (New York: Farrar, Straus and Giroux, 2000), 88.

67 Jeep Cherokee Owner's Manual, 2014, 47, https:// vehicleinfo.mopar.com/assets/publications/en-us/ Jeep/2014/Cherokee/265.pdf.

68 J. Monroe Thorington and Robert William Sandford,

The Glittering Mountains of Canada: A Record of Exploration and Pioneer Ascents in the Canadian Rockies, 1914–1924 (Victoria, BC: Rocky Mountain Books, 2012).

69 Thorington and Sandford, 3.

70 James Outram, *In the Heart of the Canadian Rockies* (Victoria, BC: Rocky Mountain Books, 2007), 15.

71 Brian Patton, *Tales from the Canadian Rockies* (Toronto: McClelland & Stewart, 1993), 208.

72 Bernbaum, *Sacred Mountains,* 86.

73 Bernbaum, 16.

74 Bernbaum, 86.

75 Ricky Jones, "Pope Francis on the Mystery of the Encounter with God," St. Ferdinand Church ACTS, accessed February 10, 2023, https://stferdinand-churchacts.org/pope-francis-on-the-mystery-of-the-encounter-with-god/.

76 Bernbaum, *Sacred Mountains,* 52.

77 Quran 42:11.

78 John Muir, *The Wilderness World of John Muir,* ed. Edwin Way Teale, illus. ed. (Boston: Mariner Books, 2001), xv.

79 Charles Bukowski, *Essential Bukowski: Poetry*, illus. ed. (New York: Ecco, 2018), 120.

80 Oscar Wilde, *The Critic as Artist* (New York: Brentano's, 1905), 201, https://babel.hathitrust.org/cgi/pt?id=coo1.ark:/13960/t8tb1pz60&seq=7.

81 Keith Waldrop quoted in Edward Hirsch, *How to Read a Poem and Fall in Love with Poetry* (New York: Ecco, 2000), 375.

82 Thorington and Sandford, *The Glittering Mountains,* 2.

83 R.W. Sandford, *The Book of Banff: The Insider's Guide to What You Need to Know to Be a Local in Banff and the Bow Valley* (Banff: Friends of Banff National Park, 1996), 175.

84 Genesis 2:18.

85 Manes, "Nature and Silence," 347.

86 David Quammen, *Natural Acts: A Sidelong View of Science and Nature,* rev. ed. (New York: W.W. Norton, 2008), xi.

87 Arthur V. Evans and Charles L. Bellamy, *An Inordinate Fondness for Beetles* (New York: Henry Holt and Co., 1996), 20.

88 "Letters Addressed to Miss Elizabeth Pelham, William Blagrove and William Pelham," *The William and Mary Quarterly* 9, no. 4 (1929): 265–74, https://doi.org/10.2307/1919380.

89 George Steiner, *Real Presences* (Chicago: University of Chicago Press, 1991), 25.

90 William Shakespeare, *Hamlet,* ed. Barbara A. Mowat and Paul Werstine, illustrated edition (New York: Simon & Schuster, 2003), 96.

91 David M. Berry and Jan Rybicki, "The Author Signal: Nietzsche's Typewriter and Medium Theory," *Stunlaw* (blog), accessed October 15, 2020, https://stunlaw.blogspot.com/2012/12/the-author-signal-nietzsches-typewriter.html.

92 Friedrich A. Kittler, *Gramophone, Film, Typewriter,* trans. Geoffrey Winthrop-Young and Michael

Wutz (Stanford: Stanford University Press,
1999), 203.

93 Martin Heidegger, *Parmenides*, trans. Andre
Schuwer and Richard Rojcewicz (Bloomington:
Indiana University Press, 1992), 85.

94 Heidegger, 81.

95 Talmud, 65b, in Jorge Luis Borges, *The Book of
Imaginary Beings*, trans. Norman Thomas di
Giovanni (London: Vintage Books, 2002), 72.

96 Nicholas Ostler, *Empires of the Word: A Language
History of the World*, illustrated edition (New York:
Harper Collins, 2005), 32.

97 Fadiman, *Ex Libris*, 90.

98 Quran 73:5.

99 Exodus 4:13.

100 Jeremiah 1:6.

101 Various, *The Norton Anthology of English
Literature*, 9th ed. (New York: W.W. Norton,
2012), 30.

102 Quran 59:21.

103 Fadiman, *Ex Libris, 26.*

SIGNS

104 Sid Marty, *The Black Grizzly of Whiskey Creek*,
illus. ed. (Toronto: McClelland & Stewart, 2008).

105 Robert Con Davis and Laurie Finke, eds., *Literary
Criticism and Theory: The Greeks to the Present*
(New York: Longman, 1989), 125.

106 Davis and Finke, 125.

SHIPS LIKE MOUNTAINS;
MOUNTAINS LIKE CLOUDS

107 Revelation 20:10.

108 Tertullian quoted in Borges, *Selected Non-Fictions*, 48.

109 Georges Perec, *Things: A Story of the Sixties and a Man Asleep*, trans. David Bellos and Andrew Leak (Boston: Verba Mundi, 1994).

LOVE IS A BURNING MANTIS

110 Bernbaum, *Sacred Mountains*, 5.

111 Terry Houston, *A Guide to Native Bees of Australia*, illus. ed. (Clayton, Australia: CSIRO Publishing, 2018), 180.

112 F. Scott Fitzgerald and Zelda Fitzgerald, *Dear Scott, Dearest Zelda: The Love Letters of F. Scott and Zelda Fitzgerald*, ed. Jackson R. Bryer and Cathy W. Barks (New York: Scribner, 2019), 30.

113 Cleanth Brooks and Robert Warren, *Understanding Poetry*, 4th ed. (New York: Holt, Rinehart and Winston, 1976), 66.

114 Cathy Davidson, *Book of Love Writers and Their Love Letters* (New York: Plume, 1996), 14.

115 Davidson, 100.

116 John 3:16.

117 Jean-Henri Fabre, *Fabre's Book of Insects* (Mineola, NY: Dover Publications, 1998), 29.

118 Fabre, 29.

119 Samuel Taylor Coleridge, *The Rime of the Ancient Mariner*, Poetry Foundation, https://

www.poetryfoundation.org/poems/43997/
the-rime-of-the-ancient-mariner-text-of-1834.

ASK NOW THE BEAST

120 Gerard Manley Hopkins, *Gerard Manley Hopkins:
The Major Works*, ed. Catherine Phillips, re-
issue edition (Oxford: Oxford University Press,
2009), 129.

121 Lewis Carroll, *Alice's Adventures in Wonderland
& Through the Looking-Glass*, illus. ed. (London:
Macmillan Collector's Library, 2016), 46.

122 Carroll, 46.

123 Carroll, 48.

124 Massimo E. Maffei and Wilhelm Boland, "The
Silent Scream of the Lima Bean," (paper presented
at Chemical Ecology: The Variety of Secondary
Metabolites Conference, Jena, Germany, June
2007), https://doi.org/10.13140/2.1.4887.6806.

125 Hirsch, *How to Read a Poem,* 42.

126 John Dart, "Woody Allen, Theologian," Religion
Online, https://www.religion-online.org/article/
woody-allen-theologian/.

127 Exodus 20:18.

128 Exodus 20:19.

MERCY

129 Kahlil Gibran, *The Collected Works of Kahlil
Gibran*, illus. ed. (New York: Everyman's Library,
2007), 277.

130 Emerson, *The Essential Writings of Ralph Waldo
Emerson,* 5.

131 David Moye, "Colorado Bear Smashes through Wall like 'Kool-Aid Man,'" *HuffPost*, August 12, 2019, https://www.huffpost.com/entry/bear-colorado-kool-aid-man_n_5d5182ede4b0cfeed1a118c4.

132 Cooke, *The Truth about Animals*, 103.

133 Leviticus 11:13.

CIRCLES

134 Jack London, *The Call of the Wild, White Fang, and Other Stories*, ed. Kenneth K. Brandt (New York: Penguin Classics, 1993), 33.

135 John James Audubon, *John James Audubon: Writings and Drawings* (New York: Library of America, 1999), 263–64.

136 David Day, *The Encyclopedia of Vanished Species* (London: Universal Books, 1989), 32.

137 Quran 2:30.

138 Day, *Vanished Species*, 43.

139 Day, 43–44.

140 Day, 50.

141 Day, 155.

142 Carl Safina, *Beyond Words: What Animals Think and Feel* (London: Picador, 2015), 134.

143 James 1:3.

144 Genesis 7:11.

145 Genesis 7:21.

146 William Shakespeare, *The Oxford Shakespeare: The Complete Sonnets and Poems*, ed. Colin Burrow (Oxford: Oxford University Press, 2008), 511.

ABOUT THE AUTHOR

Amal Alhomsi is a Syrian writer, artist, and environmentalist. He holds the position of editor-in-chief at *Oesa Magazine*. Amal resides in Banff, Alberta.

We would like to take this opportunity to acknowledge the Traditional Territories upon which we live and work. In Calgary, Alberta, we acknowledge the Niitsítapi (Blackfoot) and the people of the Treaty 7 region in Southern Alberta, which includes the Siksika, the Piikuni, the Kainai, the Tsuut'ina, and the Stoney Nakoda First Nations, including Chiniki, Bearpaw, and Wesley First Nations. The City of Calgary is also home to Métis Nation of Alberta, Region III. In Victoria, British Columbia, we acknowledge the Traditional Territories of the Lkwungen (Esquimalt and Songhees), Malahat, Pacheedaht, Scia'new, T'Souke, and W̱SÁNEĆ (Pauquachin, Tsartlip, Tsawout, Tseycum) peoples.